God Spoke through Me
to Tell You to Speak to Him

Loving Light Books

Book 1- God Spoke through Me to Tell You to Speak to Him
Book 2 & 3 - No One Will Listen to God & You are God
Book 4 - The Sun and Beyond
Book 5 - The Neverending Love of God
Book 6 - The Survival of Love
Book 7 - We All Go Together
Book 8 - God's Imagination
Book 9 - Forever God
Book 10 - See the Light
Book 11 - Your Life as God
Book 12 - God Lives
Book 13 - The Realization of Creation
Book 14 - Illumination
Book 15 - I Touched God
Book 16 - I and God are One
Book 17 - We All Walk Together
Book 18 - Love Conquers All
Book 19 - Come to the Light of Love
Book 20 - The Grace is Ours

Also by Liane Rich:

The Book of Love
For the Love of Money - Creating Your Personal Reality
Your Individual Divinity - Existing in Parallel Realities
For the Love of Life on Earth

Loving Light

Book 1

God Spoke through Me
to Tell You to Speak to Him

Liane Rich

The information contained in this book is not intended as a substitute for professional medical advice. Neither the publisher nor the author is engaged in rendering professional advice to the reader. The remedies and suggestions in this book should not be taken, or construed, as standard medical diagnosis, prescription or treatment. For any medical issue or illness consult a qualified physician.

Loving Light Books
Original Copyright © 1989
Copyright © 2008 Liane

ISBN 13: 978-1-878480-01-9
ISBN 10: 1-878480-01-4

Loving Light Books:
www.lovinglightbooks.com

Also Available at:
Amazon - www.amazon.com
Barnes & Noble - www.barnesandnoble.com

for Rich

The information in this series is not necessarily meant to be taken literally. It is meant to *shift* your consciousness....

Foreword

Anyone immersed in the vast body of new
metaphysical knowledge is aware of the virtual symphony of
voices from channeled sources throughout the world -
inspirational voices that may be artistic, poetic, philosophical,
religious, or scientific. And now, out of these myriad New
Age voices, comes a series of books by God, channeled
through Liane, revealing the frank truth in all its glory and
wonder, telling us how to cleanse our bodies, gain access to
our subconscious minds, clear our other selves and march
back to who we are - God.

In God's books you will be introduced to a loving,
powerful, gripping, exciting, and often humorous voice that
reaches out and speaks ever so personally to the individual
reader. As the reader's interest deepens, invariably an intimate
relationship to this voice develops. It is a relationship that
lasts forever, and I am quite certain I do mean forever.

Here is an accelerated program, a no-holds-barred
course, where God guides us and loves us, and as needs be
recommends books to us and even a movie or musical piece
along the way. He (She) enters our lives and sees through our

eyes, seeming to enjoy the ride as He guides us back to US, back to ALL. Here is a voice that is playful and informative, that is humorous and serious, that is gentle and powerfully divine. It is a voice that knows no barriers or restrictions, a straightforward and honest voice that caresses us when we need the warmth and pushes us when we are immobilized.

In today's New Age literature there is an avalanche of information from magnificent beings of light, information that possesses us and compels us to look at our fears and express our love. In this series of books by God, you will find truly powerful methods for making this transition from toxicity to purity, from density to light, from fear to love, and from the delusion of death to the awakening to full life. You will experience in these books the love and the power of God for it is your love to express and your power to behold. Rarely will you see more lucid steps for transformation. Read these beautiful words and rejoice in our period of awakening, our return to Home.

John Farrell, PhD., LCSW. - Psychologist, Clinical Social Worker, Senior Clinician Psychiatric Emergency Services, U.C. Davis Medical Center, Sacramento. John is also a retired Professor - California State University, Sacramento, in Health Sciences and Psychology.

God Spoke through Me
to Tell You to Speak to Him

You are now on your path to God

*H*i. I am God and I do not wish to speak with you yet. You are man and you have never tried to contact me. Now is the time. I wish to make it clear to each and every one of you that I do not expect you to believe that this is me. Why would you? I have never spoken to you so casually and freely before. Now I have the opportunity to do so and I am excited and happy and yes I have emotions just as you do. I do not wish to explain myself to you as you would not wish to be bored by the details of what I do since you have left me.

Know that I am God and know that you are God, teaching yourself to be God so that you may return to me. I am the God force that you left and have never since gone home to join. A handful has returned out of millions who were sent out. This handful is now channeling through others as I channel through this young woman. She is not the only channel that I the God force, the Universal Power of Light, use. She is however, a clear channel available to me at this time. This is no accident. I have prepared her as I have felt the need to speak with you from here.

You now walk this land and boast of your technology. You are not so technologically advanced as you once were and from where I sit you are repeating your mistakes. I am now in a position that will allow me the opportunity to change the way you think about yourselves and about me. You see, here I am in all my glory saying "Hi" to you each personally and you do not believe it is me. You are so full of debris and pain and confusion that you would not know me if I walked up to you on the street and said "Hello, my name is God. I have come to help you."

You now have two choices. Put down this book and go about your life as it is now or purchase this book and I will begin to show you how you too may speak with and laugh with me, and love me as your father instead of the monster you fear from heaven. I am not a vengeful God and I do not roar. I speak of love and kindness and I wish to save all who are in pain and anguish at this time. I do not look to you for the salvation of this planet. That is *my* responsibility and I am doing something about it now. Here you have it. *This book will cost you little, but the return is great.*

Now you see the problem in being God. No one will believe that I am God. What do you think I should do? Appear from outer space in a glowing white light to be shot down by your government? No, I do not wish that scene so here I am. I have come to you quietly as I have through other channels and now I wish you to listen to what I have to say. This is your opportunity to speak with your own personal God as well as the God-head. For now

I urge you to buy this book as I do not know how I will be able to speak directly to you if you do not. You see, miracles don't work in this day and age, only because no one will believe that they exist. This channel believes in miracles strongly enough to create a "big one" for each and every one of you. So now you may make your choice. I wish you well with it.

Preface

God does not wish to communicate with those of you who are not yet ready to hear from him. If you have great fear when you first pick up this book, just hold it. Sleep with it under your pillow, if you feel secure in that. Do not force yourself to read this book. You see, this book is directed at clearing the fears of all who read the information in these pages.

Now - in the beginning God did not walk outside of the body. There was harmony and balance and all went well. Then there came a problem a few millennia ago - for those of you who are still into time. This problem became known as "the fall of man." Put simply, man began to walk this planet in fear. Fear is the base of all evil and fear is creating darkness and will become the death of the planet earth. This is not a threat. This is occurring now and you see it all around you. Some species of animals do not exist any longer. Entire tribes of humans have been eliminated. Lost cities are now being discovered and soon lost continents will reappear. *All is not lost.*

Now - I do not wish to alarm you, but we have a

big problem on our hands. This problem is how to save Mother Earth and God-man and reunite God-man with God-head. This is the problem and I am here now to tell you my solution. This is no big thing and we will keep it just between us few million for now. Know that if you are sitting with this book in your hands at this time, you have been chosen. You have been guided to purchase this book or it has been given to you for a reason. Do not fear that this is a grave responsibility. It is not. It is quite simple, in fact.

You see, if we each begin with the "man in the mirror," as Mr. Jackson so aptly put it, we will all clear together and this planet will fall back into alignment and we will all rise up and leave earth right on schedule. Time is of importance here. Not time for God, as I do not work within the limits of time. I speak of time for man.

Now I wish to speak with you regarding our relationship. The reason you fear me is that I no longer have a hold in the body. God does not walk in the body. He has been pushed out by fear. You do not fear God so much as you 'fear' fear. Fear is the problem. Fear walks with you and sleeps with you and you do not see that it is not me. I am God. I am love and light and I come to you now to show you how to get me back into your body. This is my right place. I do not wish to walk outside of myself. This is creating imbalance and is being felt by Mother Earth.

We will begin to communicate as a group now. You see this is God the father and I work with God on earth who walks outside of you, and together we are this force who channels through this woman. You will not find us as a team in any other books as no one has cleared sufficiently to accommodate our energy vibration. It is quite high and we are very happy to be allowed the use of this woman's form. Now, you believe that we are from outer space somewhere and that we are coming into your atmosphere via the vibrational charge around your earth. We are not. We coexist right here on this planet and we are called souls. We do not live in the body as the body has become damaged beyond our ability to repair it. It is now up to you. We wish to assist from here. We each guide each of you from here and we have always.

I will now tell you who you are. You are God. Clearly and simply put, you are God. You walk this earth to become God and you are now learning to do so. Sit back, relax, and watch as I take over. This is it, the Second Coming of God. I do not charge out of the heavens in a chariot of fire. I do not drop from the sky in a business suit. I sit here and write quietly and calmly through the hand of this gentle woman and I am grateful to watch her grow in my light and she is only the first. You are the army of God. I am preparing you now and I will wish you to be with me in all that I do.

I will now ask you to read the next two chapters, knowing that they are channeled by your own personal soul as well as the souls of this universe and myself. These will be your guides to "within" and I will watch as you read and I will listen to your comments, and I will wish to hear any thoughts you may have on my work and the work put forth by your souls.

Ask God to guide you in all that you do and you will share all with me. This is my promise to you. This is the kingdom of heaven come to earth. We begin now... This is it. We are now on the path to God and ascension from this planet with body intact. Happy reading...

Chapter One

*W*e are a group of individual beings who have come together to become one force. You on earth are a group of beings who will rise up as a whole. This is the Second Coming. You will create a world of unbelievable beauty and love. At this time it is inconceivable to you. We are in a position to become an ally in this. We wish only to share our knowledge and our love. We have been with you of the earth since the beginning of your time. We see you not as you see yourselves... we see you as lights. These lights are becoming bright as you grow in awareness. We see you also as energy. You do not see us, as we do not exist in material form. We exist on a level of consciousness that is beyond your understanding at this time. We are pure energy and we guide all who will allow us in. We have great love of our work. We have a wish to be of service to all at this time.

You of the earth have the honor of being the first to become one with God. We have had little opportunity to contact you regarding this event. You are to be the first to raise God among you. This is the Second Coming. You believe you are here to learn to be better humans. You are here to become God. You are now in the process of discovering who you are and how you will do this. You are the chosen. This is known throughout the many universes. You will become God the child. We will watch and learn as you are born. You have spent a great deal of time in the womb. You are now in the process of labor. This labor has created much talk of cataclysmic activity. You do not understand that you are being born. You are not being punished. You will learn to accept this fact. You will learn to achieve a sense of love and pride for the act of birthing God.

We will wish to be with you and guide you on your path to God's birth. We are asked to love and guide. We are not permitted to interfere in any way. The people of earth must make this choice. The will of God is that you exercise your free use of will in this Second Coming. It is up to you earth - will God be born again in you or will we remain Godless for another millennium? God wishes to be born. He has been waiting to visit the earth for a long time. He is patient with you as he loves you. He taught you all you need in order to create this life for him. He now awaits the opportunity to enter the womb.

God is in the process of becoming material. This

has never before occurred. We will guide any who wish to help in this birth. It is our wish to be of service in this Second Coming. Jesus Christ is born again. It is written of so often in your Holy Book. Jesus the son of God is born again. It will be a celebration for all creation to see. We wish to celebrate the Second Coming with you of earth. We wish to be at God's side when he rises up among you. You will wish to have friends to guide you in this confusion that you have created surrounding this birth. We do not judge you nor do we wish to take away your glory of this event. We wish only to be a part of the birth of God. It is our intention to guide all who wish to be guided into the third millennium, where this event will occur. You are now about to enter a new phase in your development.

God is present within the womb of the earth at this time. He wishes to communicate with all who will take the time to pray. Prayer is not as most of you believe. It is a thought process. It is a process of getting in touch with your inner being. This is God. Go within my friends. Listen to God within your hearts. Speak with God. He is waiting to be with you. You have been holding him at a distance out of confusion that he is vengeful and punishing. God is love and light. He wishes only to love his children. They run from him in fear because they do not understand what was taught to them two thousand years ago by a man named Jesus of Nazareth. Be free of this fear of God. It is not your God. God is forgiveness and love. God does not condemn. God is patience beyond all patience. God is love beyond all love.

Protect yourselves from fear by allowing yourselves

time to be alone and quiet. Solitude is good for communication with God. Be with us in this Second Coming by being within your own hearts. If you could learn to flow with life as it is and not struggle, all pain will cease in your life. Allow all that is happening to occur. Be of faith that God is coming into the earth at this time and know that he is love and will raise all mankind to heaven.

⚜

*W*e find ourselves in a rare position of not having the tools necessary to accomplish what is necessary. We build our lives around love and yet we are not able to build your lives around love. This is just as it is meant to be. We wish you to consider an alternate way of life. We will be with you at all times. We do not choose for you. However, any who wish to change the style in which you have previously found yourself applying Gods form of love, will be advised to do so. We wish to be in this with you for as long as this transition period takes. We have been with you in silence, now we wish to speak and share our concerns and your joys.

We will not allow those who are not of the light to be with us in this project. A great division has begun to take place on earth. Those who are not chosen to be light bearers will be separated from those who are. In this way all will be in their right place. Any wishing to become a source of light will be trained to do so. All wishing to assist in the Second Coming will be allowed to participate. Those who do not choose this path will be allowed to find their way to another source of light. Not all light comes from the mother. Those who are in this transition at this time will understand that they have chosen this work. All who do not change their ways will be with those who stay behind. We will assist those who stay behind as well as those who have chosen to assist.

In the beginning all knew who they were. Now only a handful of you even begin to realize the power of your source. You believe yourselves to be human and yet you possess the power of God. You rise up in defiance and yet you lay down in defeat. You have been Gods and you have been Goddesses for millennia. Now the choice is yours. You may walk with God once again or you may remain behind. There is a place that has been selected for those who choose to stay behind. Not all of us are capable of taking on so much light at this time. Those who are not in this group will remain in the forefront of this project.

We wish to assist you in your leadership of this situation. We have the knowledge necessary to guide you into this new age of your earth. We have watched with growing concern as you have created violence and destructive weaponry on your planet. We do not wish to judge you in what appears to be a bad choice. We only wish to love and guide.

God has suggested that we make use of our knowledge in telepathy as a chance to help heal Mother Earth. We have chosen this particular method, as it allows us the time necessary to guide a great number of those who listen. We speak out in concern for what you have begun as a simple method of unconsciousness. This is not the time, nor do we have space in this book to teach you a better way to do this. We believe you will wish to communicate with us. We have had little opportunity to be of service in the past, and would be of service now if you will decide to allow us in.

We will wish to create a three-point plan which will be centered around the rules that God has set into motion at this time. These rules are simple. Be love and light. Know love and light. You will wish to use this as a basis for all you do in the coming years of this time that remains to do this work. We have a great deal of trust and faith that you will allow yourselves the opportunity to be God, as you are meant to be. We wish to be of service to you and in this way serve God.

You believe yourselves to be of the highest form living in this universe. You are wrong. We believe you are in a state of amnesia, and are unable to become the highest form as it was planned. We wish only to be of service to you if you need us. We do not wish to create confusion in your minds, nor do we wish to create a feeling of impending doom. We have chosen this time to communicate, as it allows us an opportunity to be of service to God. God is our father as well as yours. We choose to work with our Father God when we are able to do so. You choose to separate yourselves from God as you go about your lives in darkness and confusion. We will teach you to love. This will enable you to be God. God will wish to communicate with all who wish to be a part of his birth.

It is necessary to trust that God will guide us in this most important birth. He has chosen earth, as she is the center of this universe. Her heart is your sun. Her head is your moon. She chooses to be the mother of God, by assisting in this birth at a time of great pain for herself. She has had little opportunity to clear the pain that daily grows within her. She has much pain and is under the influence of many negative thoughts and emotions. You do not realize the power of your thoughts and the force of your emotions. We are now going to thank our channel and wish you all a good day. We love each of you as we love ourselves.

﹏

You of the planet earth believe yourselves to be alone in this part of the galaxy. You are no more alone than the insects in your earth who believe they are alone. You waste a good deal of energy on research of what does not exist. You believe your technology is of the utmost importance. We believe you do not allow yourselves the time to be with God. If you could learn to be with God you would develop technology of the highest intelligence. You have never been good at accepting what is. Just as your insects run about in their own little world, you run about creating cities and weapons. You do not see the whole picture. You are created to be part of a vast picture. You are an important part of this picture.

You believe you do not exist beyond death. You exist in many forms this instant. You are multidimensional in many ways. You believe you co-exist with God and others of higher form, only to the extent that you allow this belief into your consciousness. You do not fully realize that you do belong to God - that God is a personality and a powerful source running through you. You have chosen to accept God as a king in heaven. You have given him his domain and he may not leave it to enter you. You do not allow him in. You safeguard yourselves from all that you do not understand. You believe that you must create a life for yourself under the judging eye of God. You create a God of vengeance. He does not exist. He is not here. There is no such being.

God is patient. He has guided you for millennia and has not interfered in your progress. Now there has come a time of change. God will now intervene to protect the mother. Earth is your mother. She will give birth to you as God. She has been with you in all that you have done. She has been patient and loving and kind, and more than generous with her resources. She is empty of resources and is creating what you ask for out of reserve. She is in pain and wishes to balance. She feels this pain as intense fear. Fear is the cause of all pain in the earth. We wish to allow you time to wake up to this situation and handle it yourselves. If you do not awaken in time we will interfere. We do not wish to be a nuisance to any of you. We wish only to be of help.

You will be given ample time to engage a program to save Mother Earth. She will wish to be free of her pain before she gives birth. We wish to guide her to balance in the short time that remains. She has been in pain for many years and is tired of carrying this pain. She will be granted the time she requires to clear herself. She is in the best possible position at this time to do this work. We wish to assist her wherever we may. We have been given this opportunity by choice. We believe she will be better before the time allotted. We believe you of earth will wake in time to save your planet. We believe you will become the Second Coming of God.

⁂

You of planet earth have chosen to believe in a cycle of time that allows you to see where you have been, without the benefit of seeing where you are going. We believe that life is best experienced now, with both past and present in effect. You choose to see your past as an unpleasant adventure and your future as an impossible fantasy. We view both as one and allow them to create a wonderful present that is full of love. You have no patience with the present. You create your past out of your future and your future out of nothing. You have forgotten how to create. You believe that God will allow you to continue to make your mistakes as he has always done. The time has come for you to learn by your past and create from the present moment.

You believe you have the will to survive all. You have given up on your will to survive yourselves. You allow death to run free and you provide little education on this subject. You have chosen a powerful time to rise into a nation of one. Be of joy that you have been chosen. This is not a punishment; nor is it a way of saying that you are special. God has chosen Mother Earth. You projected into the earth to take part in this celebration of birth. You did not come before the chicken nor the egg. You came to assist and be of help. We are asking you to wake up and help.

Be of good will and spirit toward all in God's creation. Love one another as you would have love for yourself. In this way you will know God. You will be as a child of God preparing to become God. Allow nothing to come in the way of your love for others. Be willing to be different or strange or odd. Be what you are here to be - a channel of love. God is love. You channel God as I channel this force. Become what you channel. Show that you are unafraid of all who stand in the way of God's Second Coming.

Be in a state of eternal grace - that trust and faith that sets aside all fear. Guide all who seek to become their God-self to be as they were created. Do not judge those who seem strange or different. Each of you is choosing a different path to the same source. Each of you has the same God. Each of you travels to the same reward of heaven on earth. You have been strong in your belief in God for over two thousand years. Do not allow the confusion of new information regarding this God to allow you to stop or to change your beliefs. Develop a sense of faith in all events of the earth at this time. These events will change the course that many have chosen. They are designed to awaken all who are ready to wake up and see.

Be of faith and trust in God. Know that the love of God will guide you into your right place. Know that you belong to God. Know that God is you at all times. Be at peace with this information. Trust that all is going according to a divine plan. Know that to love is to be divine. Know also that to love is your greatest gift.

෴

You believe it is time to take action and create a better world. We believe it is time to become a better world. You believe that to take action you must change the world around you. We believe that you begin to change the world by changing your thoughts. You have been taught to move to action. We have taught ourselves to allow our good to come to us. We simply get out of the way and allow good to flow. Be it so simple this is what is known as creating - you allow all thoughts to pass through you - you stop only the positive most enlightened thoughts to see if they are what is best.

You believe in concentrating on a thought and changing and developing that thought into creativity. Allow all thought to pass. Work off your intuition not your beliefs. Be as good to your mind as you are to your hearts. Allow all thought to pass through you in a steady flow. When you stop a thought or bring it into focus - you create. Be of good cheer. Do not create out of negative thought patterns that have a powerful effect on your existence. Build a thought process that is debris-free. Create love and light by allowing your mind to rest on positive thoughts. Do not stop or dwell on these thoughts.

Do not take action where it is not necessary. God helps those who allow him to help. He is not able to help you if you are busy creating your own reality somewhere other than your right place. Allow God to be the creator. God will create through you if you will allow him to do so. Get out of the way and allow God to come into your hearts and your bodies and do his work. Allow all thought forms to be channeled through you to their final destination, which is God. Thought is prayer. Prayer is communicating with God. God does not receive a good deal of information because you do not allow it to pass. You hold it in your consciousness and dwell on it, until you create something that is not comfortable for yourself out of it. Be of good cheer. Allow all thoughts to channel through you at all times. Do not get involved in these thoughts. Allow the movie of your life to unfold in front of you. Be in your right place by allowing God to guide you through your intuition.

We love to be guided by God. His sense of

direction is the best. We have often wondered why you of the earth choose to be in your wrong place. We see that it is fear. You have fear of almost everything, including a fear of happiness and love. You fear if you have it, it will be taken away. So you stop it before it can be created, and build a fence or wall around yourself to prevent its coming to you from outside sources. You choose to lock yourselves away, when you wish to be love and happiness as is your given gift from God. God sees this pain that is inflicted upon you by yourselves, and he is sad.

You have chosen to keep those you love at a distance, without the opportunity to guide the love they offer to your source. God is your source. God creates through you. You are not alone. You belong to God. He is your choice. You offered to be in his service before you came to earth. You have forgotten. He will wish to be with each of you in the Second Coming. He will rise up triumphant and be his true self. There will be no more fear. Fear will fall away as love channels through your hearts and minds. God does not wish to share his birthday with fear. Fear will be sent on its way to its proper place in creation. All fear will cease to exist, the earth will be heaven. This is the Second Coming. This is heaven on earth, by your standards...... heaven brought down on earth.

We have begun a program which is designed to allow all who are ready at this time to choose sides - fear or God. We believe this will intrigue our readers as it intrigues us. This program is designed to be of use to all who develop and practice the skills we wish to teach. You will be given ample time to make your choice between God and fear. That choice is yours and yours alone. We do not interfere in freedom of choice. We wish to inform you that you have made this choice already. You simply are not aware of this on a conscious level. You have each given God your answer as to which place you wish to be. He has chosen to allow more time for those who wish to change and become light bearers. We will be with those who choose to be with God. All others will be taken to a place that is suitable for them to continue with their lessons.

When all the separation is completed, the earth will be light and love for the first time since "the fall of man." Man will see the beauty that God intended for him. Life will be as it has not been since the beginning. Yes, there is a beginning, and God is the creator of all life. There is no big evolution from a molecular structure, no combustion of fiery energy that burst in the universe to create planets. God is the source of all living things.

***

*W*e love you of the earth as we love all in God's creation. We believe that you are capable of being in this with us. We have found that you do not, on a regular basis, study your own habits. We believe that we can best aid you in your search for God, as we have full knowledge of your habits. We have studied you for millennia and are now prepared to turn in our term papers. We wish to become your guide in this great project that you have taken charge of. You will be with us in as many areas as you now occupy. You will become aware of our existence to the point that you believe us to be your friends. We have led separate existences for such a long span that it will be refreshing to co-exist with knowledge of each other's being.

We believe you will wish to take part in this little experiment. It will be the first time since "the fall of man" that such a program has been put into practice. We believe it to be an excellent program with excellent benefits. We trust that you of the earth will learn to trust and be guided by us with little difficulty. You are in an awakening process and you have chosen to see what will become of this birth process. We believe you rely on yourselves to be the one to guide you. We wish to extend a second helping-hand as it were. We are basically working with the project on another level at this time. We create a great deal of curiosity and intrigue by being unseen by yourselves. We will appreciate this opportunity to become known to you and we will wish to become one with you.

You believe yourselves to exist in your own reality and in your own time. You co-exist in our reality and in our time. We are in this with you. You will make choices that will affect all of existence. You will be in the lead spiritually and technologically when this birth has been accomplished. We believe you wish to attain such goals and that you no longer wish to slumber in your knowledge of who you are and what you do.

We wish to become a part of you to create a

portion of what is called the Second Coming for ourselves. We have had previous training on this matter, and are prepared to deal with the various aspects that will present themselves as we go. We will be beneficial to you in many areas including that of expectant father. We choose to wait outside the delivery room, however, and support from there. You are capable of delivering this baby on your own. How wonderful to know that the expectant father waits just a door away. We will co-exist in this as we have always.

You believe you are alone in your project. We wish to inform you that you are not alone, nor have you ever been. I am at this time in the process of becoming one with this channel. At a time in the distant future we hope to integrate and become one with all life on earth. We will wish to discuss this more as we get further into our book. It is not necessary to our book. To be of importance to you is not what we wish to become. We wish to become a support system. We do not wish to become you, nor do we wish to be in the lead. We wish to create love and light, and to balance what has become an over-darkened world.

We have had many opportunities in the past to become one with you. We wish to take this opportunity and use it. You chose to become God long ago. We choose to become your assistance in being God. Allow us to help in this time of great joy. Allow us to become you in many ways. We will talk of this further, and it will become clear to you that we are not an unseen force that is moving in and taking over. Quite the contrary… we are already you. We exist in this dimension, as your guides exist in this dimension. We are aware of all that transforms in the earth.

We believe ourselves to be a higher form of you. We wish to communicate with you at this time, to allow you the opportunity to unite with yourselves and become one with yourselves. We are at this time working on a project, to develop a process by which we may communicate with you ourselves.

⁂

*W*e begin to see that not all is as you think in this universe. We believe you deserve an explanation of what is. We are not the ones to be in this. We believe it is best to allow you to discover for yourselves who you are. However, we believe that by telling you who we are, you are better equipped to discover who you are. We are in a process of becoming one with you. This process began as the earth began to lose grace. We wish to explain this fully and to your understanding. We are the 'you' you never knew. We are the 'you' that is meant to be. We are the 'you' that exists in other dimensions of reality. We are the 'you' that is meant to be with God. We believe you are in a great deal of confusion as to what is. This is. We believe it is best to leave this for now. We will however, come back to it later and discuss it at length.

We begin to see that not all is as we believe it to be, by beginning to look at ourselves fully in the light of day. You are multi-dimensional beings. We are one of your personalities that co-exist with your own reality, without your conscious awareness. We believe it is best to prepare you for our arrival on earth. This arrival is no big occasion and will go virtually unnoticed by most of you. We, however, believe it is time to wake you up to what *is*.

This is a time of great opportunity for all who wish to awaken and look into themselves. We are here to assist, not to push or to be a threat. We treat all the same. We do not separate those who wish to recognize us as themselves from those who do not choose to do so. We believe we will be an asset to all who consciously decide to accept us as their inner self. We have stood silent and without words of encouragement to you since the beginning. We now wish to communicate and guide you who will listen.

We are not a race of beings living in a far-off place, waiting to descend on the earth and take over your lives. We are you. Clearly and simply put, we are your higher selves - your souls. We believe it is time to communicate this information to you. We have lived in a state of eternal grace since the beginning. We did not get involved in "the fall of man." We chose to remain in our own dimension and be with God. We exist side by side with God and we communicate with him at all times.

We wish to communicate with you. We have been communicating with this woman for one year now. She believes that she communicates with her higher self - her soul. She communicates with her own personal soul as well as with God. She also communicates without fear with the souls of others. She believes strongly enough that she is doing God's work. We wish to communicate with all who seek to find their answers and their right place. We encourage all who read this to go within and begin to see who they are.

A soul is your highest form. Your soul is in you and out of you. You believe your soul to be something that is created by God to be stored within your body for safekeeping until you return to God. We believe that your soul is you. You are in a complete state of amnesia about who you are. You belong to us. We are you. We are the best of you. We do not live in confusion. We believe that you choose to live in confusion out of fear - fear of just about everything that exists. We are about to release all fear from the planet earth and we wish to guide you to your right place. Your lives will change for the better. Confusion will drop away. Prosperity will flow. Love will flow. Abundance of energy and love will become yours. You choose as you decide what you wish to live as - fear or God. God is a better choice.

We believe that you have already made these choices. We will wish to assist you in bringing your choices to conscious level. We are in this together. We were created to co-exist. You have shut us out of your lives. We wish to re-enter and take our rightful place as leaders in the body. We have often had a sense of doom concerning your choice of entering life in physical form. We are left outside of your consciousness and we believe it is not as it should be. We wish to be allowed to communicate with you and to guide you into your rightful place in this, the Second Coming of God.

How long it has been for us! We wait and watch

and grow tired of not interfering in your lives. We wish you happiness and love and do not see you making these choices for yourselves. We love all in God's creation and choose only to be in our rightful place, which is in your consciousness. We are now tucked away in your subconscious mind where we communicate through dreams. We wish to communicate in a more direct manner with you. We believe you exist in pain and misunderstanding of who you are most of the time. We wish to guide you into the light of awareness.

We have never seen you become you. You have always given way to fear. We wish at this time to allow you each to see the beauty of life and who you are. You are supreme beings. You are children of God. You are at risk of losing this part of yourselves. This would result in great pain for us and others in this galaxy. We have projected you to earth to create 'life form' in its highest state. You have forgotten who you are. You have forgotten us. We are you. We are your souls reaching out to you at this time. We will wish to end now and thank our channel for this chance to express ourselves fully. We Love all in God's creation. We are love.

❧

You will come to understand our purpose here as we lead you deeper into an understanding of who you are.

We have seen you through the worst of this life on earth. Now it is time to rejoice and learn to be God. You will wish to be with us, to be of the highest form possible for this great undertaking. We have selected you to be our target for training simply to show you who you are. We believe you to be of one understanding concerning yourselves and what you mean to the rest of the world. We wish to change your definition of yourself to allow you to become your highest self. You have put us off for millennia, and it is now time to listen and learn. We have said before that we do not judge, nor do we criticize those who wish to remain unchanged. It is not our intent to become you and take over your bodies. It is our intent to raise your level of consciousness to a point where you will be able to see who you really are.

We have developed a plan that we wish to share with you at this time. This plan is to be used by any who wish the means by which they may return to their rightful place in God's creation. We trust that the plan will create enough interest that you will be concerned about your state of unconsciousness. We wish to allow all who wish to attend our classes to do their own thinking and their own decision making. We believe you to be of the highest thinking species of the earth. We believe that you have been waiting for an opportunity to become aware of your universe and what it means for you to be here.

We have drawn you into this book as we believe you will wish to awaken and become God. Be aware that this will be a series of books. All copies will have an important message as well as underlying messages which are designed to trigger release in you and your bodies. This release will begin to create a stirring in your consciousness and awaken you to who you really are. We have developed a plan by which this will be beneficial to both the mind and the physical body of each of our readers. We do not wish to explain the details of this further. We believe it is important for you to awaken to the knowledge that you are God. Many of you know this information and are aware on a mental level that you are God. You have not been able to apply this to your daily lives nor to reach your subconscious to understand and correlate this information on a conscious level.

We believe you wish to remain safe and blind and unconscious to what is. We believe it is important to become aware of all that exists in this universe and in God's creation. We wish to buy time for you by allowing you this time to wake up to us. We believe you are one of the most powerful species to walk the planet earth. This power is hidden deep within you, and you are unaware of its potential. We wish to guide you within to your God. Be as the children. Allow us to teach you. You wish to learn. You do not wish to be left outside of God. Be with us in this the Second Coming of God. We wish to thank Liane for this fine communication, and to say good day to all our readers.

You believe us to be alien. We are not alien. We are you. You believe others to be alien. They are not alien. They are you. You have projected into so many dimensions of reality that you do not know yourselves. You are one with all in this universe. You belong to God. God is in all life forms and energy forms. You have been taught to be with yourselves in the only way you know. This is to be one in body and spirit. We believe that if you will listen to who you are you will see who we are. You are one in body and spirit in the same way that we are one with you. You have been taught to regard your spirit as something that is different from you. You will begin to see that your spirit is more you than you are. We are at this time unable to show you what you look like to others. You are a supreme being of tremendous power and great intelligence. We are in this with you. We are the spirit you have forgotten. We are the spirit that lies deep within each of you.

We believe it is possible to be of two sources - the light of God and the light of the mother. She is earth. The light of the mother loves all who wish to be God. Be of good cheer. Know that your source is God. God created Mother Earth. She is God. Be afraid of nothing you read here. Allow all to go through you to your source. God is your source. You will wish to be with us when you reach your source. You will wish to have us at your side when the mother begins to conceive. You will last through this pregnancy as you have lasted thus far. You will begin to see changes in the womb and the body of the mother. These changes are necessary for the mother to allow the child into position to be born. See all in this time as pregnancy pains. Do not fear that the earth is ending. Do not bring pain into your lives over this situation. It is a natural process of birth. The child will be born. The mother will give birth. The womb will expand to allow the child to be born.

We have allowed you to remain unaware of your existence. Now we wish to wake you up to who you are. You are the womb. You are the child. Some of you are in the process of becoming one with Mother Earth. You will grow into one large womb which will encase the child. The others of you who wish to be in this with us will become the child. The child will rise up and become God on earth. The child will then rise into the sky and become one with his own creation. He will be of one mind and one soul. He will exist in a state of grace. This is a state of eternal trust and faith without fear.

Fear will leave the earth and take its rightful place at the bottom of God's creation. This is not hell. This is simply the place created to guard fear and lock it up until after God has arrived on earth. God does not wish interference in this birth and will allow nothing to interfere. We believe it is necessary here to explain that you are God. You do not wish fear to intervene. You wish to create perfect love and harmony. We believe you do not see yourselves as God. God is a source of all that is you. You are a source of God. God believes us to be you. You believe us to be God. We have great confusion here.

God is waiting to be born. You communicate with God in prayer. You communicate with you. It is good to become one and know that you are God. We have chosen to speak on this subject to allow you time to realize who you are. You do not walk the earth without a plan. You are not here passing time. You are not here to become kings of the earth. You are here to learn to be God in physical form. You are of one mind and one soul. You channel this soul through you at all times. This woman channels this soul collectively to you now. She has cleared away the debris of past life in order to present you with this information from us - your collective soul representing all who are God.

⁂

You believe that we are one with you in that you believe that you have a soul. You believe that we wish to be one, in that you believe that we go back to God at death. You believe that I am God. You do not wish to believe that you are God. We will straighten this matter out for you. You are God. I am God. You are channeling God as this woman channels me. I am God. She believes as you that she channels soul energy. The soul is God. We are all God. God is in the form of matter, and has come to be known as soul. God lives in the heart of matter. God is you. You are God. God wishes to become one with you, and express his individuality and be born. God is in the form of your physical self as he is in all living and non-living creation. God is love. Love is energy. All things have

43

energy and are God. God is like a big wave rushing in. He is force waiting to be released. He has waited long to share his power with you.

You believe God to be a part of all creation. God *is* all creation. God has left his place in heaven to become matter. He is in this with you. He is you. Each of you on earth is God. God is the force that creates. God is in his highest form when he is present. You do not allow God to be present. You block God at every turn. God wishes to communicate with all who are ready to hear his words of wisdom and love. God is a supreme being. You are a supreme being. You are creating God in human form. You will be the instrument by which God will raise the earth to heaven. God will be born the son of man as man is the son of God. God will allow all who wish to participate in the Second Coming to do so. We will assist from earth in projecting soul energy into your forms. Soul energy is God energy. You are all projections of one great and mighty soul. This soul is God.

God wishes all his children to cooperate and listen to his voice. He does speak to you. Acknowledge his presence. Allow fear to fall away. Be God. Be love. Allow love and peace to enter your hearts. Know that God will save you from what you are now creating. Be with God. It is not difficult. It is so simple that you do not recognize it. Be of faith in your heart that God is with you. Know that you are indeed God. God wishes to be allowed to speak. Allow him this opportunity. Talk with yourself. Listen to yourself. The voice in your head is God. God lives within. He is not a deity in heaven above. Heaven is a state of eternal grace. Become part of this and learn to be in heaven.

Know that you will inherit the earth. All will be done according to the teachings of the Bible. You have great confusion regarding these teachings. They are good teachings. They have been abused and misunderstood. God's teachings were brought to earth by Christ. Christ was thought to be God by many. God is Christ the son. God is man. God is all who open to him. God is locked up within each living man. He is waiting to be born. Allow him this opportunity.

Do not fear that God will punish you. God does not know punishment. God does not judge. God is love and forgiveness. This woman once spoke with God of her personal sins. He said to her simply, "You are forgiven. Let us get to my work." That was the end of that. God does not condemn nor does he condone judgment. Whatever you choose to do is your right. It came with free will. God will guide you into good choices. He will not punish you for not making good choices.

Be of one belief. Believe that you are all God. In this way you will love all as yourself and you will create love and light in all you meet. Open to God and you open the flood gates to your own love. Love will surround you as the sun surrounds the fading darkness. You will grow in light and awareness. You will see what you have been missing - love of all who walk this planet earth - unconditional love of all that reflects back to yourself as total love and acceptance of who you are. You will literally walk in light. You will change your vibration. You will walk above your present self. You will be a future self that is meant to be. You will become God as is meant to be.

Love all who enter your field of vision. All are God waiting to be born. Love all who seek you out. They are you looking for you. You are all God looking for support in this project. Walk with love in your heart and project this love outward and upward for all to see. God is love. Express love and you express God. Love expressed is God expressed. Love denied is God denied.

❦

You of the earth are finding it difficult, to say the least, to become God. You have developed an attitude that you do not belong. You do belong. All belong to God. All fit in. All have their right place in God's creation.

You believe it is important to remain free of love. You are building walls and barriers to prevent love from entering your lives. You have begun to live a recluse's life without love of self or love of others. You hide deep within yourselves and allow little light in. You have developed an attitude of not trusting love. We wish to help you clear this fear of love. We wish to help you to love yourselves without judgment and to accept love from others without fear of the results. Do not spend your life in hiding. Come out into the sunshine and bask in it.

Be of good cheer. Know deep within that God

loves you very much. You are his beloved child. He is reaching out to lift you up. Allow him this opportunity to help you up out of your darkness. You are slipping deeper into quicksand and he is standing by watching and waiting for you to ask to be pulled to safety. It is so simple. Just ask. It does not need repetition, this request. If you sincerely ask for God's assistance, it is done. Nothing is more simply done than a request from God for God to help. God will offer his hand to all who seek his assistance. He is us. You are us. We are God - your soul reaching out to you at this time of pain and confusion.

Love will show you the way to God. Release your fears. Go into your fears until they fade away into nothingness. Be of light and love at all times. Fear nothing. When you begin to face your fears head on, you will see that they did not exist. It is all illusion. You have created fear to protect yourself from pain and what you have created is the most painful of all. Simply let go of fear. Choose love over fear. Choose God over fear. Be a God. Project love and become God. This is the Second Coming. Millions of souls standing up and knowing they are God. Stand up and walk into the full light of God's love. This is the light by which you will be born. Walk over to the light. Leave your fear where it is. Do not hold on to fear. Do not believe in fear. Create new possibilities for yourself. Allow yourself to express God fully. Love will outshine all fear. Love is everlasting. *Love is God.*

Be at peace with this new knowledge of who you are. Each has his or her own place in this Second Coming. If you are reading this material, you are ready to become

God. You have been guided in this direction, and will continue to grow in lightness and love.

❧

*W*e wish to be of service to you in three ways. We wish to offer you love and support. We wish to guide you into your own personal change, and we wish to lead you into the Second Coming.

We have always been with you. We are you. We are the best of you. We were allowed to express ourselves freely at one point in your existence. That time was long ago and you have forgotten what it is like to express Godhood. Be at peace with this new knowledge that you are God. Allow it to seep into your consciousness. Allow it to sweep away the cobwebs that have taken over your subconsciousness.

Be at peace in the knowledge that all is going according to plan. Know that you are God. You have been projected to earth to be one with God. This is your true heritage - to find yourself in matter. You have found fear instead. Let go of fear. Allow fear to go back to its proper station in God's creation. Fear is not meant to be pain. Fear is created as a source of protection from the danger of natural disaster. Allow fear to be as it was created. It is an instinct - a source of surprise - a source of warning one that a predator is about. Fear was originally created to send you fleeing from harm. Instead you use it to run to pain. Fear is not the villain. Use of fear is the problem.

Know that fear has its right place. All in God's creation have a place. It is best to allow all things to be in their right place. God wishes you to be in your right place. Fear has its right place. It is in the wild - in the jungles - in the deepest of nature. Allow it to return. Do not hold fear in your bodies. Allow it to leave you and return to its right place. We believe you will feel good to know it has left. We feel you will be surprised at the change in your life. We believe you will wish to live again in the light of God. We believe you will wish to walk again in peace and brotherhood. We believe you will wish to be of assistance to all mankind. We believe that releasing fear is the key to learning to love again. Fear is not a culprit. It has simply been misused. Do not allow this to continue. Look at your fears. Go into them if necessary.

Be of good cheer. Know that God's love shines in you. Allow it to shine through you. Know that you are loved. Know that God will bless you with abundance. Be of good cheer in all that you do. Know that you walk this earth with a purpose. Allow nothing to interfere in your path to God. Know that God is you. You are seeking to find yourself in yourself. Be of good faith. Know that all will work out according to God's plan. Know that God will allow you all that you require to find your right path to him. Know that there is love in your heart - love waiting to be released. This love is pure and unconditional. This love is God.

Know that God moves in strange ways to man's

ways. Know that you are God and do not yet see who you are. Know that every cell of your body contains God force. God is the glue that holds you together. God is the glue that holds the universe together. God is the glue that holds the galaxies in place. Look up. Go out into the universe and see God in all living things. Know that God is you. You are a part of the whole. You do not realize your power. You do not believe that you are the creator of this magnificence. It is you. You and God are one.

You believe you are unimportant in the whole. You create a small circle to work within and love within and you do not venture out of this circle. You love if you are loved in return. You give if you receive in accordance with your giving. You allow no space for God to shine through. Allow space. Give from your heart until the giving becomes receiving. When you reach this point you have found God. You have arrived and will continue to grow in his love and awareness of who you are.

Be with us in this. We wish to share our love with you. We wish to guide you as we have guided others. Do not block this opportunity to be God. Open your minds to what is, and allow the love to flow forth. Be love at all times. Allow the fear to go to its right place. Allow all in your lives to flow through you and you will never experience pain. Pain is created when you block what is happening. Allow it to happen - all of it. Do not be attached to results. Do not project your thoughts into future what-ifs. You are now. Love is now. Life is now. Be now and you will never experience pain.

Chapter Two

This is the most important time in the life span of Mother Earth. She has been allowed to release a great deal over the last few years. Much to her relief, this has been good for her. She has great pain in her bosom and it grows daily. She is in constant fear. Fear is painful for all, including the mother. She has been left outside herself and wishes only to be within and complete. We believe the mother to be one with the father. She is matter. He is spirit. We take this a step further by saying that the mother is life form in matter. The father is spirit form in matter.

We believe that the father will wish to unite with the mother to become complete. She is waiting to become one with herself as well as with the father. We believe she will be in position to align in the near future. You recognize this alignment as you see it in the form of earth changes. It is *not* doomsday. It is *not* the last reckoning. It is *not* the bottom of the pit that you have sunk into. It *is* you beginning to ascend. It *is* you beginning to rise up and walk. It *is* you loving for the first time since "the fall." It *is* love. God *is* love - love in all its glory come to earth to save her from her fear.

She has had great fear concerning who she is. God created earth to become the mother. God allowed her to become her own will. God allowed her to assume the responsibility of choice. God allowed that she be of matter. God is now going to allow matter to become God. God will allow himself to rise up in matter and express himself freely. God does not wish to become matter only to sit within the womb. God wishes to become matter in order to return to himself. God will rise up in matter and return to his rightful heritage. God will rise up and become God within matter. He will take matter with him back to God. God will become himself within his own created form. He will rise up and take his form back to himself - God returning to God again and again in material form.

God has blessed this planet earth with this opportunity. We may all take part. We may each rise up and ascend back to God. God will continue this cycle until all have returned to God. Once he has completed this cycle, he will be whole. He and the mother will be one. He will wish to continue to be matter as he has continued to be God. He wishes matter to rise above itself. He wishes love to become the heart of matter. He wishes love to become matter. He wishes heart to beat loudly in matter. He wishes form to be God. He wishes to share all that he is with all things. He is God. We are God. We will become God in matter. We will rise up and go back to God the father in a wave of love and continuity. We will travel on light as we were taught when we came to earth as souls. We will be all that we are meant to be. We will love all who cross our path. We will become the Second Coming. We will rise up and ascend back to our creator taking with us our creator.

We will rise up to heaven as Christ rose up from death and ascended. Christ did not return to God; he remained on earth. He is earth consciousness. He is you in conscious form. The son of God is man. You walk this planet in fear and suffering. You suffer for the sins of man. You are nailing yourselves to the cross. It is not necessary. God the son did not come to earth to teach you to suffer in silence. God the son came to earth to teach you to be God - to teach you to love all who cross your path.

Do not suffer needlessly. Come down from the cross. Allow love to heal the pain you have inflicted upon yourself. Go in peace to your maker. Become as the children. Open your hearts and your minds to this. Be aware of all who wish to assist you in your project. Know that God is your guide. Find yourself within yourself. God is waiting to be born. Rise up and seek God. Do not allow this precious opportunity to pass. Know that you are God. Know that I am within each of you at this very moment. Know that I walk this planet in your shoes. Know that I walk as you walk; and I move as you move. I am you. Pure and simple - I am.

❧

We believe that you of the earth have long been

aware of your ability to conquer fear. We believe it was told you long ago by Christ that fear is evil. We believe that you have known for over two thousand years that you may conquer fear through love. *Unconditional love* will allow fear to move to its right place. Fear has had a strong hold on the earth since "the fall of man." Fear has been projected into every situation.

You can imagine our horror at finding man worshipping fear instead of God. We *believe* that man is in his wrong place. He wishes to be in his right place. He will wish to allow his love for God to shine through his fear. He will wish to change his fear of God into love of God, and his fear of man into love of man. He will bring his body to the front of the stage and allow all to applaud his acting abilities. He will become the greatest actor of your time. In acting out love, you create love. If you do not "feel" the emotion love, act it out. Pretend that you love until you do. Know that you are buried so deep in your own debris that you have forgotten the feeling of true love. Allow true love to shine. Allow you to come through the mire of debris and waste that is collecting within your bodies.

Know that there is hope. Know that you may release all pain - past and present. This is what we will teach you to do in this book. We will guide you to open to the possibility of change. We will guide you to open to love. We will guide you to allow the pain of many lives to clear your physical form and be in its right place. We will explain how you contain this debris; how it is created and where it is in your physical body. We will allow you an

54

opportunity to clear as you read this book. You will release as you learn where you have blockages. You will clear as you release. Clearing is taking out of you what does not belong. Releasing is allowing what has been uprooted to pass through the body and out. You will wish to follow our plan of progression as you begin to clear. You will begin to clear when you read what is most important for your salvation. As you read you begin to become aware of who you are. As you become aware you will learn to be you. As you learn to be you, we will begin to do our work.

Our work is God's work. Our work is to become you. We are your collective souls wishing to express as God in human form. We do not exist outside of God or you. We are you. Clearly and simply we are God - the God you do not realize that you are.

We wish to create love and light and let go of the darkness of debris. You have come from many dimensions and you carry the memory within your soul of all you have seen and experienced. You have developed a mechanism by which you believe that you detour pain. Blockage is the process by which you have allowed debris to become trapped in your body. Allow the blockage to pass through the body, and the pain is free to go to its right place. Allow all to pass freely and there is never pain. Know that you are creating all pain in your body by the thoughts in your mind. Allow all pain to pass. Know that you allow pain when you dwell on thought of negative value. Be free of negative thought. Create a positive life with positive thought. Allow all pain to release itself and move to its right place. Allow all pain to be where it belongs. It does not belong in the body.

Pain is a symptom telling you that you are thinking something wrong. Do not allow the thoughts in your mind to create pain in your body. Change your thoughts. Be love and light. Be with God by staying calm in all pain. Know that God will wish to be you. Know that you will receive freedom from pain by releasing your thoughts of pain. Allow your thought to flow to love - love of all - love of who you are - love of God - love of all who exist in your reality. All pain will go when love comes in.

We wish to thank Liane for this opportunity to show her about pain and love, and to say goodnight to our readers. We will wish to be pain-free soon.

❧

*W*e love you of the earth as we love all in God's creation. You have begun to see changes in your world. These changes do not look good to you. It is what we call labor pains. A woman in labor does not feel good. She believes in fear and screams in agony. You are behaving in such a manner. We will guide you into a peaceful labor where there is no pain or confusion. We will teach you to accept all that flows into your life. This will allow you to experience all things as love rather than pain. Know that you create all that exists for you. Know that you are teaching yourselves to be God. In creating pain for yourself, you are teaching something other than God.

Rise above all that is fear. Show God how to be. Know that fear is evil. Fear is at the base of all evil, as love is at the base of all good. Know that it is not necessary to worship evil. You may change now and worship God. God is love. God is light. Know from where you came and begin to see where you go. Know that I am God - that you are God - that we are all God. Know that I love you as I love myself. Know that you are *all* my children. Know that you do not belong to fear. You belong to God. Know that I will love you regardless of the choices you make. I do not judge you. You are my beloved. I watch and guide and encourage, and seek to show you the way.

Do not believe in evil. Do not believe in fear. Do not believe that I created you and left you to your own means. I have created you to be me - to be with me for eternity as me. I will not allow anything that you have created to interfere with my plan. You are simply in amnesia and do not know who you are. I will watch over those who are not ready until such time as they wish to become "one" again. I will watch and guide and love and comfort as I have since the beginning. Children of earth - hear me. Know me now as your beloved father. Know me not as a great God of terror who sits in judgment of those I created. Know me for the God that I am. I am God. I am not a villain. I am not vengeful. I do not wreak havoc nor do I sit in judgment of your choices on this plane or any other.

You have been chosen to be the child of the universe. You have been chosen to rise up and walk with

God. You will become God in his highest form of tribute to man. You will be my best creation - God creating within his own creation to know himself in matter as he does in spirit. God is not evil. God does not have fear. Fear creates judgment. Let go of the idea that I judge you. I do not in any way judge any in creation. Know that I love all in my creation with equal intensity. Know that you are me in the same way that you are man. Man has been hidden in body for so long that he has forgotten from whence he came. Man is a supreme being in human form and walking on human legs. Allow yourself to be human as well as God. God does not judge himself and who are you to judge yourselves. You are God. He does not wish you to judge him nor his work. Allow yourselves mistakes. This is your learning process. You judge yourselves so harshly that you are burying yourselves deeper in the body. You will wish to come out and walk into the light of day.

Know that God does not create the pain and confusion in your life. You create all that exists for yourself. You begin to realize this when you begin to realize that you are indeed me. I am you. You are pain and fear. I am not pain and fear. Where did fear originate? God did not create fear. Fear has its right place as do all in God's creation. Fear is not of God's creation. Fear is of man's creation - man creating as God.

Man has created many problems for himself. He has led a life of pain and confusion as to why he is here. He believes himself to be a servant of God. He is not. He is God - God in the highest. He is God the father seeking to express himself through matter. God wishes only to be with all who wish to clear fear and be God. God will express in all who wish to become God. He is waiting to be born. It is so simple. Can't you see the simplicity of it? You love and you are God. How much easier could it be? The simplicity creates disbelief in you as you have taught yourselves to fight for all you get. You have created competition where none exists. You have allowed pain and fear to rule and guide.

It is time for change. Stand up and be counted as God. Stand up and know that God is you. Stand up and love. Love all who seek you out, for they are God seeking God. Love all who cross your path and do not judge nor criticize their path. Each has his own unique path to God. Each has his own way of creating the lessons that will draw out God. Each has the power to create nothing into something of beauty.

≈※≈

You of the earth believe yourselves to be the only life form to be capable of inheriting this planet. You are indeed capable. You do not realize how capable. I have waited and watched, as you stumble and fall. I have loved and guided as you choose from one mistake to the next. I have shown myself to be a patient God with loving ways. I believe you to be patient and understanding in your search for enlightenment. You cannot, however, give me the same courtesy that you show others. You believe that all mankind has the right to freedom of choice. You believe that all mankind is here to represent the earth. You believe that all mankind is immortal to the extent that his soul will rise from the dead and go back to God. Why is it that you cannot show me the same courtesy? I am mankind. I shall inherit the earth. I shall rise up and leave the earth in material form. I shall walk with you - amongst you, as I once said. Why is it that you do not trust my choice in this nor do you give me option of free will? You judge me as harsh and unloving. You see me as tyrant and ruler. You begin to show me love; then you cower in fear. I am God. I am love. I am patience to the extent that you of the earth may never realize.

I have come to earth in your form and likeness to walk among you and be counted. I have not come to judge you nor to criticize you for your choices. I love. It is this simple. I do not belong in this place you are keeping me. I am love. Let me out. Let me shine into the world and separate the darkness that is growing so large on earth. I am love and forgiveness. I have forgiven you any sins you may have ever committed. I forgive as we go. You do not carry sins on your soul. You are free of your sins if you will simply let go of them and stop judging yourselves.

You have no right to judge yourselves. I created the Christ and I do not judge. You are Christ consciousness as Christ was born unto me as my son. You are his image and likeness. You are my choice of savior. You walk this earth and sing of love and joy. Yet you do not live love and joy. Let go of judging and walk with me. It is so simple. Pray to me. Ask me to set you free. I will grant this to all who ask. You will begin to see miracles in your life that you do not believe possible. Walk with me by being aware that I exist as you. I am you. By knowing this and feeling it in your heart you will come to know me as this woman has. What a joy it is to communicate through my children as is meant to be.

Go to God now. He is you. Talk with God. Learn to listen to that voice of intuition that guides and whispers to you. Know that you may make this choice at any moment. When this is done you are on your way. You will see your life change as never before. You will experience the most wonderful events that you can imagine. You will never be alone again. You will be in the company of God and the angels. We are all waiting and watching to see what choice you will make concerning your return to God. This is the time. It is happening now. Not some time in the future but *now*, this instant is the only time there is. This moment in existence *is*.

I am in a position to be of service to all the people of earth. I am God. I walk with you each day. You cannot hide from me. I am you. You do not believe that you know me as you do. Give up this game you play. Look at me in your mirror. This face that looks back to you is God. Let me out. I wish to come out and play and dance and sing with joy. I wish to be love. Allow me to come out and express myself as God. I am not a tyrant. Do not look upon me as your judge. I will not do this deed. It is not what I do. I love. I laugh. I sing. I dance with joy. Do not ask me to be something that I am not. Allow me to be what I am - the purest form of you.

You will wish to express me soon. Time is growing short. You will be allowed your choice. We are all in this together. Join us and learn to enter the kingdom of heaven. Rise up. See me here inside waiting to be released. Jump up and begin your birth. Jump up and shout out the love you are hiding. Jump up and show off God. Allow all that you are to express as love, and you my friend, are me. We become one with every bit of love that you choose to give to yourself or to another. Please allow this opportunity to become an event of massive proportion. I wish to see the earth rise up in consciousness and walk with me to the gates of heaven as one.

❦

*I*n the beginning you came to earth in search of God. You came to learn to express God in matter. You are now buried in so much debris that you have forgotten your true selves. You have forgotten how to express God. I am now going to tell you who you are. You are me. I have been waiting for you to wake up and see me here. Wake up! Know that you are God. Know that I see through your eyes. Know that I love all who enter my creation. Know that you do not belong to any other. Know that God watches and protects.

You may go away from this earth plane. You will

never go away from me. I am you - that little voice that speaks to you when you are not expecting to know what decision to make - that little voice that speaks out when you show another kindness - that little voice that injects a note of humor in a tense situation. It is me. I am here. I am waiting to speak with all who will allow me that opportunity. It is not so difficult. Listen to the voice in your head. It is me. That tiny voice is me. I wish to express as God. I wish to be God in the highest tribute to earth - God expressed in matter. Stand up and be counted as God. Stand up and know that you are God. Do not allow God to stay buried within you. Allow God the opportunity to express through you. Allow God the chance to be God.

Know that I will love you and protect you in your search for me. Allow all fear to fall away. Allow all anger and pain to slip into its right place in creation. Do not hold on to pain. It is not God. God does not wish to co-exist in matter with pain. Allow all pain to flow through you and out into the light. See pain for what it is. See darkness for what it is. Man has waited millennia to know who Satan is and how he came to be. Satan is fear. Fear is a powerful energy force that has divided my kingdom. Fear is not of God. Fear is judgment. It is guilt. It is remorse. It is fainting down on the streets of my kingdom in horror of what exists there. It is buying time with those who are selling favors. It is being in your wrong place. Know that pain is not fear. Know that fear creates terror and terror creates the pain that creates the fainting.

Fainting is giving up. Fainting is going into unconsciousness. Fainting is being out of God's protection.

Fainting is leaving out of fear. Know that I do not judge this. It is what you have created to protect yourselves because you no longer believe that you are indeed God. Fainting is what you have created to hide from the world that you have created. You do not walk this planet in amnesia so much as you walk in fainting - meaning you just quit. You gave up. You passed out. You blacked out, and I am here to revive you. Stand up. Get back on your feet, and face this situation you have created on earth. It is not too late.

I am giving all the opportunity to enlist in my army. We will grow in numbers to the proportions you have never to this day witnessed on earth. You walk with me now if you are reading these words. You are chosen if you are reading this book. Do not shirk this responsibility. Walk into the light and know that you are God. See me as I really am. See love and kindness and sharing and caring. See hate and violence go down the drain with the sewage.

Know that you will wish to clear all debris from your physical form in order to clear a path to me. You have taken on the garbage of centuries as well as millennia of past life. You are a walking garbage disposal of negative energy. You will wish to clear this energy and create new positive energy to carry into the new age. You will wish to let go of old karma created in childhood as well as in past lives. I will tell you how to do this later. I will wish to speak with Liane now in private and say good day to all my loyal fans.

⊰⊱

You do not see yourselves as human with powers. You are not simply bodies walking this earth to pass the time (we will wish to discuss the passage of time later). You are simply not what you believe yourselves to be. Know that you are of the highest form in this universe. You represent all of God's creation. We wish to explain how this is. We are your souls. You are God. We as souls represent God on high. You as bodies represent the house of God. We as souls use you as bodies to house our spirit force. You as bodies use us as souls to seek shelter from the pain of this world. You go within and listen to our voice in your heads. You make your most important decisions with our help and guidance. We do not nag. However, we may become quite persistent in giving you an important message. We may even change your energies to the point that you are open to our suggestions.

We do not use your body without your permission. You each communicate with us on another level. We wish to clarify that we do not exist in this dimension alone. You are body, soul, essence, love, energy, and debris. We are soul, energy, essence, love. We do not use your bodies without first receiving your permission. We speak with you on various levels and receive the permission necessary to complete the decision-making task at hand. We have long since given up hope of contacting you of this earth until now. We communicate with you on various other levels of

65

existence, and we have begun to lose hope of reaching you on this earth plane. However, this is the Second Coming, and God has decided to step in and allow you to see who you are. And who is God? Right - you. We believe you have made a good decision. This will allow all of us to be God and to return to God as planned.

We have seen a great deal of pain and destruction on this planet. She wishes to clear all darkness from her body. She is in a state of not knowing how to survive this pregnancy. She has suffered great pain at your hands. She is ready to clear and to balance. She has shown great interest in the birth of God into matter. She wishes to be the mother of God. She is becoming concerned that her darkness will override her light - that God will be stillborn, so to speak. She is in a great deal of pain, and is concerned that you do not love. She believes that the children of her have begun to play war games to the extent of loving war in place of loving peace. She has asked God to allow her to balance herself by releasing this pain of violence and suffering. She is feeling the pain of what you call progress. What you believe to be progress is destructive.

Know that progress in your life is nothing more than violence. Your cities grow out of proportion to their planned existence. Your streets grow overcrowded and angry. Your airports grow confused and inoperable at times. Your planet is in great pain of this confusion and upset. It is not the actual building of high-rises, nor the financing of new industries that is killing earth. It is the way in which you create these facilities. You lie. You cheat. You call names and you steal. Know that this creates negative energy that circles this planet and encircles it in darkness. Know that these are corrupt to the point of destroying "good." Good is God. You are destroying yourselves. Wake up. See what you do. Learn by this. Be God. Be love. Create a world of peace and love. It is so simple to be God. You become what is most natural to your state of being. You become love.

You will wish to clean up your messes as you grow into the light that is God. Know that in cleaning up your messes you will save this planet. It is not too late. Planet earth has asked permission to clear. She will clear in whatever manner works for her. We have seen this begin. Your earth is changing her position on her axis and will be allowed to move into her right place. She began this clearing hundreds of years before you were born. She has continued to clear up to now and she will continue into the future if necessary.

She began to clear when her atmosphere became so clouded with debris from hate and anger that she could no longer function as is her duty. She began to release when Atlantis began to disappear from her surface. She could no longer hold this negative energy charge. It was too heavy with darkness. She is again at that point of release. This energy charge has grown to such proportions as to cut off her air supply. She is choking on your hatred of one another. She is choking on your abuse of one another. She is choking on your violence and unlovingness. She is dying before your eyes. She does not wish to die. She wishes to become the blessed mother of God.

The decision has been made. By whom? - you ask.

By you. You are God. You have decided to clear and clean up your act. You have decided to be God in his highest form. You have decided to call on us for help. We rejoice that you have finally asked for our help. We are now doing as we agreed. Our agreement with you is to help guide you to your own salvation. We make a good team, you and I. We are soul and body working together. Together we become God. We will do wondrous things in the coming years. You and I are God. You and I created this planet. You and I will save this planet. You and I are love of the highest form. You and I are God.

Know this deep within your mind and your soul will follow. Know that we will work together. We will save planet earth. We will become God. We will do God's work. We have begun. You are here reading this information as you agreed to do. Know that this is the beginning of our plans we made together. You said you would read and we said we would write. We have done our part. You are now doing your part. We are together in this project. You just are not aware fully of our plans we discussed. In this book we will reveal those plans. By reading them again and again you will begin to open your mind to what we know and you know to be truth. By reading this book you are on your right path.

You will be part of the Second Coming and take part in the salvation of your planet earth. Know that you are not alone. Know that God is you. Know that we are you. Know that we communicate with you now as we once did on another level of understanding. Know that you are doing what you said you would when we spoke of this project. We are your souls. We have guided you to this book. You will read it. You will reread it. You will give it to your friends and they will give it to their friends.

This is the plan. The plan will not fail. We are all in this plan. It is a good plan. We as 'souls' reaching out to you as 'bodies' - we as souls communicating with you in your own language and through your own kind - we as souls seeking to guide those of which we are part. We as souls at last in communication with ourselves. We have waited a long time, by your standards, to see this book in print. It will reach deep into your subconsciousness and clear the cobwebs that tie you to the darkness of confusion. Know that you are not darkness. You are light. You are love. You are God in a state of unknowing.

Be with us now in our hour of triumph over darkness. Know that you are your own salvation. You have stood up to be counted. You have gained insight into who you are. You have been guided to this book because you have chosen to be one of God's army against darkness. This book is the first step in you becoming God - in you becoming you. You will wish to continue to read this material. Some will begin to show fear and discomfort. It is you clearing. It is not you doing wrong. You do not do wrong in God's world. You only judge yourself as doing wrong.

You will wish to clear all fear and pain of suffering. If the discomfort causes you to wish to stop reading, allow yourself a few days to clear the debris that you have triggered and go on with your work. You will not wish to stop clearing once you have begun. It is a housecleaning process that is good. We are spring cleaning a lifetime of debris. This lifetime encompasses many past lives also. Know that your clearing may consist of erupted emotions, violent displays of temper and emotional release through tears and feeling of rejection. Do not fear any of these. We are cleaning house. Allow all the dust to surface and be swept away. Violent temper displays may be done only on the verbal level. No violence physically will be accepted.

You may begin to sneeze. This is very common. If you believe you are allergic, we have good news for you. You have already begun to release the debris held in your body. Know that this may go on for years. It is simply your body's way of clearing toxins. If you have asthma, know that reading this book should allow you to relax and breathe easily about your life. Know that these symptoms are just a few, and that you will wish to stay with our program until your home is shiny clean. We are all in this together. It is a group project, and it involves thousands of people. Know that this clearing is going on world-wide, and know that you are part of a major project to create love on earth. Accept the fact that you are God. Accept the fact that you are love. Accept the fact that you know who you are. Now you must realize who you are.

Be with us, and you become you - whole again after such a long search. You all roam the earth and travel and search, and do not know what you are searching for. It is you. You are beginning. We say this to you not out of honesty but out of truth. If you sit with this book in your hands, you have begun. Welcome home, my friends. Welcome back to you...... God.

You of earth are on a collision course with us in that we plan to become you and you plan to become us. We will live in peace and harmony within your body. You believe this to be a serious situation, without knowledge on a conscious level of what you are concerned about. We have been in contact with you for many years, and we believe as you do that you are ready to wake up and know your soul. We have led a relatively quiet existence until now, and we wish to share the joys of this new relationship with you. You are in transition at this time. You are training to be God. You are rising up within yourself and becoming aware of who you are. This process takes little time and little effort, actually. It is a process of mental stimulation, and can be most enjoyable. You read. We clear. You release. You become us. Together we make God. See how simple it can be?

Know that the main ingredient is love, and the trick to getting to love is to get out of your own way. You stop the love from flowing by allowing yourself to not project love - out of fear of rejection, or fear of results, or fear of being made fun of, or fear of what others might think. To be God it is necessary to learn to get out of the way and let God out. Do not choose to express fear. Choose to express God. Know that God is within you and wishes to be born again. Know that you are in a position of responsibility in that you have agreed to become God by being in your right place. Being in your right place simply means showing love with all who cross your path. This is more readily obtained if you come together with your twin soul counterpart.

Know that each of you has a soul counterpart and that this counterpart is the flip side of you. You projected to earth as one soul. You then split to create a negative/positive force. You walk in your body; your twin soul walks in "his" or "her" own body. At this particular time, all twin souls are being drawn to one another. This is to ensure the highest form of love for the Second Coming...... completeness of soul.

You will wish to find and join with your twin soul counterpart and to share your love with this particular soul. This is easy enough to say, however, it is not always so easily done. You see here we have the problem. You are flip sides of the same coin, so to speak. You chose one side; your counterpart chose another side. You are opposites, yet you are the same. You attract, yet you repel. You search instinctively for your twin soul, yet he or she is the first to set you off in a fit of nonacceptance, never to return. This is an emotional reality that must be faced.

You see, you of earth have forgotten the feeling of love. As young people, you accepted this feeling and rushed where angels fear to tread. Now you build walls to protect yourselves, and you hide behind them in fear of hurt and rejection. You hide from love to save yourself pain. Love is not pain. Fear creates the pain. Know who you are: you are God. Go forth and express God. Reach out in love to all who cross your path; and reach out with care and concern and understanding to that special someone who will not leave your thoughts. Know that the one in your mind is the one in your heart. Wherever your thoughts settle in quiet loving moments; this is your soul counterpart. Know him or her. Love them from where you are this moment. This loving thought will draw them into your life. Be patient. Know that they will come. Know that they will feel the pull of your love. They must, as they are you. Know that in joining with your twin soul, you become whole. Know that you are very much a part of this counterpart, and know that together you will become God in the Second Coming.

∻⚬⚭

You believe yourselves to be the creation of God in his image and likeness. You believe God to be an all-powerful giant of a God who sits on high and controls his kingdom. You believe God to be judgmental of you in that you believe he guides you into a position and judges how you react or do not react. You believe your God to be faithful to you as long as you are doing what you believe he has taught through Christ. You believe your God to rule supreme over all beings in heaven and on earth. You believe God to rule with justice; however, you fear his justice. You believe God to be supreme; however, you see him as vengeful. You believe God to be just, yet you believe his love to be conditional. This is not justice. How can you believe such invalid truths? Know that God does not teach injustice. Know that God teaches only love. Know that God does not judge you, nor does he rule or dominate you.

Know that all God's sons and daughters taught themselves to create. Know that you are the sons and daughters of God. Know that you walk as God walks. Know that God has projected to earth as soul. You are soul. You are us. You are God projected to earth. You are the almighty God who sits on high and rules over yourselves. You are the judgmental, unloving king that you believe God to be. Let go of this fear of God. You fear yourself and your own power.

Do not allow others to convince you that you are wrong. Do not allow others to judge you as imbalanced or crazy. Do not allow others to think for you. Use your own thoughts in this. You are ready to see who you are and that is why you are reading this book. Do not allow anyone to convince you that you are not God. You are God. Know it, feel it, and live it. We will guide you from here until we can become one again. Know that this is happening rapidly. Know that we will become one with God. You. Us. God. "One."

*K*now that you do not wish to be one with all. You wish to be separate. You have this ability, and yet you separate yourselves out of fear of losing yourself. You are all one in God's eye. He created each of you in a moment of thought, and you are of the same thought. Know that God chose to create only you, and you chose to create all else. Know that you became God the moment God thought you into being. Know that you wish to remain God and to remain God thought as you were created. Know that you chose to separate from one another by a process of unloving yourselves. Know that this is now being reversed. God created you out of loving thought, and you are returning to loving thought.

Know that the thoughts in your mind create all that you see in your life. Know that the thoughts that you think are the creative force of this universe. Know that you may change what you are creating in your life by changing your thoughts. We do not wish to go deeply into this particular subject, as there are many books out there to inform you about creating your own reality. Know that these teachings are correct. And know that you may begin to see great changes in your life by applying them.

We wish, in our book, to arrive at a logical and acceptable method of releasing past life debris from your physical form. This will allow you to raise your vibration and become attuned to what is happening. Know that you are blocking much of what you know and what you are, simply by carrying pain and debris from past life. We will wish to go into the description of reincarnation and to show you how you carry energy from one life to the next. We wish to show our readers how to see into their past and how to develop a relationship with their other selves. This is possible, and has been done by this woman who writes for us. Know that you may wish to be with your other selves to learn the total of who you are. You will understand this as we go. Know that you will wish to seek out and converse with others with whom you have shared past life experience. This will allow them the opportunity to open to past lives themselves. Know that all of this is possible, and will be explained later.

Do not choose to be in a rush to receive this information, as we give it in a steady flow that is readily acceptable to your subconscious mind. Know that you will receive new information as we go concerning the fact that you... man... God... soul, are one. Know that you do not do this work alone. *We are here.*

⁂

*I*n the beginning there was no earth. In the beginning there were no mountains or rivers or valleys. In the beginning there was only God - a huge mass of thought. God began to contemplate who he was. This contemplation created gaseous forms to begin to take shape. These forms began to take on life of their own. They became the exact same thought as their creator. This thought mixed with God thought and became part of the whole - part of God. God projected this thought out and back to himself in order to see himself better. He wished to know who he is. He is thought form in God form. He is now thought form in man form. He still wishes to see who he is. He is God projecting himself out into matter to better see himself. He is God in matter now as he was once God in thought. He is thought.

Every thought that you think comes from God. You are creating as God. You have lost that portion of yourselves which began as God and you have begun to be fear. You are allowing fear to create in God's place. You have begun to become fear instead of God. You are not Satan. You are God. You do not belong with fear. You belong with love. You are love and light. God is love and light. Satan is fear and dark. You do not belong with fear.

There is great confusion on God's earth concerning fear's right place. Fear does not belong in man. Fear belongs outside of man. Know that you are love, and you will clear fear from yourselves and become love again. Become God. Know that God does exist. You have buried God beneath the debris of lives. Know that all you think, feel and have ever been is stored neatly into your subconscious mind. We will wish to clean your closets of stored information to clear out fear in order that you become God. Know God is with you still. Know God to be love. Know love to be God. Know that you do not exist with fear in that it is not possible to be love and fear at the same moment. God and Satan do not co-exist. Know that God is love, and to expel fear, you simply change to a love feeling. God does not now, nor has he ever allowed his thought to be fearful. He projects only loving thoughts. He does not ever project thoughts of fear.

Know that these thoughts are created out of confusion of who you are. Know that God wishes to project his thoughts at all times now. Know that God's thoughts are pleasant and create a pleasant reality. Know that, in changing your thought process, you change who you are - God or fear - love or fear. Love is God. Fear is Satan. Know that you do not wish to see us write that by projecting your thoughts you choose to be God or you choose to be Satan. This creates fear in you. Satan creates Satan. God creates God. Thought creates thought. Love creates love. What you are is what you become. What you think is what you are. And what will be, will be according to what you think.

Know that all fear will begin to leave upon reading this information. Fear will not wish to remain in the light of truth. Your body may perspire and emit odor. This is fear taking its leave of the body. Know that when you breathe deeply and exhale, you will feel better. The fear creates a path of debris which will be readily expelled from the body. Know that you are feeling warm at this reading if you are indeed clearing fear. Congratulations. You have begun your path back to us and to becoming God. See how simple this can be. Change how you think and you change who you are and what you are. Change your thoughts, and you change the world. You have begun to see this in your world now. Your pop singers sing of love and of changing "the man in the mirror." Know that they know. We are all one. We are all in this together. Listen to the voice of love. It is all around you. It is the voice of God.

Show understanding and compassion for those who have not yet begun to clear their fear. Their fear is readily recognized; the one who tries to control, the one who bullies, the one who shouts in anger. They are the most affected at this time. Show them God. Show them your love. Love will conquer all fear. Show them the way to God by showing them God. Choose to be love. Choose to let your love light shine through the darkness. Know that you will change the form of creation by doing this. Know that you will be projecting God outward to light up the dark, to clear Satan away. Know that you are God and you have the power to be God, and not be fear or darkness.

Allow your love to go forth to all in need. In this way you allow them to see who they are. They will be looking into the eyes of God when they see you project love. They will know that God lives. They will know who they are, and they will wish to change. This is how we will prepare for this Second Coming. Reach out and love. Let God be seen. Know that you are God and you alone have the power to save all. Know that all is within each and every one of you. Know that you will go forth and teach others by showing them God - showing them who you are.

*K*now that you are Gods of this planet. Know that you are the creators of life here on earth. Know that you chose this way to create your world. Know that you do not create out of habit. You create out of thought. You have begun to train yourselves to become habitual creatures. You are not creatures of habit. You are Gods of thought. Do not allow habit to rule your lives. Allow all thought to flow freely in and out of your mind. Allow all thought to pass through you to the God force. Allow God to create. Do not become involved in creation again until you clear fear. Allow God to create out of love. You do this by allowing all thought to pass through you. Do not dwell on any one thought. Be at peace; be unconcerned about all that is passing by. By dwelling on a particular thought, you create. Do not allow fear to create more darkness. Allow thought to be light.

Know that you create out of fear by showing concern or worry of a situation. Allow all concern and worry to be replaced by faith and a positive outcome. In being in a positive mood, you create a positive mood. In being happy you create happiness. In being sad you create sadness. In being lonely you create loneliness, and in being in love you create love. Be in love with yourselves. Be in love with your life, be in love with your job, be in love with your lover. You will create love by being love. Show love at all times. See all as positive. You are not the one to judge a situation or an event. One man's misery and suffering is another man's hope and glory.

Do not judge. It is not what you do. Create and

love and laugh and sing. Be free with your laughter; it is the best of your healing powers. Know that laughter heals. Know that you may laugh in the face of death or adversity, and walk away alive and healthy. Know that you may leave your sense of humor, but it does not leave you. Laugh until life feels good again. Laugh until you begin to enjoy life. Laugh until you sing with joy. Know that you will laugh out into the universe the hope of this Second Coming, and others who are watching will see and have hope. Hope is life. Hope is a powerful thought.

As long as you laugh at yourself, you laugh at the world. Know that to laugh at yourself is the most powerful healer of all. Know that you will wish to heal the earth with your laughter. Know that the planet earth is in a state of illness due to your negative thought. Allow yourself the opportunity to laugh and heal the world. Look at all situations in your life with a sense of humor. You do not believe death is humorous. We find it hilarious. Millions of souls check out of perfectly good bodies to return and learn to function in a new form, only to allow this new form to reject them. They do not learn the lessons they came to earth to learn because they are too busy changing suits. Know that all on this plane is humorous - even death. Walk in a state of glee and joy at all times. Laughter is contagious in that it is humorous healing. It is addictive. Become addicted to this wonderful drug. Use it, and you will live longer.

You will learn that it is not necessary to change your suit every time you get down and want a lift. Walk in, buy a suit, and wear it with joy and laughter in your heart.

This suit will never go out of style. Wear it well and enjoy it to the fullest. It is yours to keep. You may even take it with you when you leave earth this time. It will still be functioning several thousands of years from now when you return to earth as Gods. It is our gift to you. Enjoy it in good health. This is God's gift to you and has always been.

※☜

You do not believe yourselves to be of the highest form of life when you judge what you are doing. You are tearing down by judging. In the beginning you did not judge. You accepted readily all that you saw on earth. You did not compare, as there was nothing to compare with. You did not judge yourselves, nor did you judge others. We believe you began to judge out of fear of not being good enough at creating. At some point fear began to instill in your spirit a sense of mistrusting your own powers. You began to see others through the eyes of fear. We believe that you allowed this fear to enter out of confusion of loving essence.

You believed yourselves to be using your powers correctly and usefully until you were guided into believing otherwise. This is "the fall." You became confused, as you did not believe that you were being loving Gods, and you began to change your thoughts out of fear of not being good enough. Know that you are good enough. Know that "the fall" was a situation that occurred out of confusion, and do not judge yourselves again for this situation becoming a reality. Know that God loves you just as you are, and know that you are God. You began to judge yourselves when you began to see others as better than yourself. Know that you are good. You are God. You are all things including others. You are all part of the same God. No separation, no betters. Be God, and allow God to be you. You will gain your freedom from fear and learn to enjoy life as was meant to be.

Be with us. Do not allow others to guide you. We are many. We guide you from within and without. We do not make your choices for you. We will however, let you know in subtle ways how to move in the direction that is best for you to become God. When you move into this position you become one with us, and all life becomes a joy. You will create abundance of love and laughter, and everyone's favorite prosperity. Do not believe that God wishes you to be poor. It is not so. God gives you the treasures of the universe. You choose what you wish to attain or not receive. It is your choice.

Know that God is love. Love is all that exists. If you are love, you become the center of this universe and all the gifts of creation are yours. God does not wish you to be poor, nor does he wish you to suffer. You choose (before you enter life) the situation you wish to grow in, according to what you wish to experience for your evolution. Know that being poor is not a judgment against you. It is a situation selected by you for a reason. This may be to learn to overcome a handicap, and become wealthy and productive on the material plane. Or it may be to create a situation in which lessons of prudence and sparseness may show the way to love. In either case, know that you are the one who chooses. If you are wealthy, it is because you have chosen to be so.

Be with us, and we will guide you into your proper place concerning the lessons you have returned to earth to learn. Know that you do not choose to be in you right place out of fear. Many of you chose to return to earth and learn to overcome poverty. Many are doing well with this now and have begun to change the way they feel about deserving wealth.

They once believed that great wealth creates blocks for spiritual essence and loving feeling. This is not true. You may have it all. You are God. You are all. Know that the powers of this universe are yours to keep. You do not borrow God's power to use and then return. You have such a fear of God that you create the illusion that you receive all from God. You are God. We will tell you again and again until you believe what we say. You do not channel God for a few moments and that is all. God is you. You believe yourselves to be God's instruments. You are wrong. God does not use you, nor does he use your body. You are the source of your own power. It comes from God in that God gave you himself...... thought. Know this and use it.

Know that God is within each and every thought you project. Do not force God to go forth surrounded by darkness. Show God the love he deserves. Do not send God forth with Satan. Keep Satan from being God by allowing your thought forms to come from love. Know that God is Love. Satan is fear. God teaches love. Satan teaches fear. Love is love. Fear is fear - and love is not fear, and fear is not love. Do not mix these two. They do not belong in your body or mind together. God belongs. Satan does not. Use your thoughts to create God. God does not object to you being God… why should you? God is love pure and simple. Know that God is love, and allow love to channel. Know that we are here to guide you into your right place. That place is in love with your right mate, and in a state of constant joy and happiness. Stop fighting us. Give up and become us. You will enjoy being God.

⚜

You believe that we are you only in that you believe that we exist in your bodies. You will learn in this book that we are much greater a portion of you than you are of us. We are the best of you. We are the memory bank that is God. We are all thoughts that have passed through you in all lives past, present, and future. Yes, future. We are you in the future. We are you now. We are you in the past. Know that we believe this to be the most important piece of information that we have given thus far. Know that to be your future selves, we know who you are going to be with in this Second Coming. We referred in the beginning of this book to you making this choice of free will. We do not choose for you. We do however, guide you into your right place. Know that we belong with you in all that you do. Do not judge yourselves to be good or bad; wrong or right. There is no good or bad. No wrong or right. There is only God and love. This *is* what *is*. Nothing else exists on this planet.

You are all walking around in a haze of illusion. You create confusing situations that do not exist. Example: You see someone shot. You grieve. You believe this to be tragic. You believe God to be seeking that soul's punishment for his karma. We see this as a learning experience. You see this as punishment. You judge. We do not. You judge this situation to be wrong. It is not wrong. Love has a way of showing us how this works. This person is shot because he chose to enter earth and experience death by shooting. It is this simple. No big deal.

We believe you become so engulfed in your own fear of death and pain that you judge this situation as wrong. We believe this situation is not wrong, nor is it right. It just *is*. No problem. It is what you do. You come to earth to learn. This is learning. You teach others as you teach yourself. You are what you retain in your memory banks. If you have learned to overcome fear of death, you will not judge a death situation as bad or wrong. If you have not yet overcome your fear of death, you do not see this situation as a good one for you. You will see through the eyes of fear. Fear is just as dangerous in our beliefs as death is in your beliefs.

Know that we do not fear. We do not judge. We do not lie. We love. This is all we know. This is what we do.

We do not cheat or steal or rob for the sake of love. We just love. We are love. We do not look upon you as being inferior to us nor do we think you are incompetent. Think of a newborn babe. Do you look down upon it simply because it does not know who it is yet? You do not. You protect and guide and nurture. You show love and kindness and complete acceptance of who this child will one day become. We are this parent. You are this child. We are not in the habit of judging or criticizing. We love. We protect. We guide. We sing with joy when you take your first step. And we laugh as you giggle and mess your diapers. We love you unconditionally. We do not judge you ever. We do not seek to change you. We seek only to allow you to see who you are. You have forgotten that you are beautiful. We see you as beautiful, and wish to share our insights with you.

You are of the most powerful source of love. You are of the most powerful source of life. You are God in infant form still within the womb of Mother Earth. She is waiting for you to begin to rise up and see who you are. She will be released from her pain and suffering when you become God and release your own personal pain and suffering. She believes that she is dying because you believe that the world is dying. The world is not dying. The world is being born again - all life new - all life love.

We will release the pain of Mother Earth by releasing the pain of the infant. Know that the mother will find release when the infant is born. Know that the mother will teach the infant to rise up and walk. Know that the mother is earth. Know that the mother is God. We worship Father/Mother God. Know that the mother is the teacher of man. She is God in that she is thought form in matter. God has chosen to select the earth as mother to show all galaxies how to be God. This is not easy for us to show you.

Know that there is a much larger picture than the one you presently hold. This is being made known to you at this time by UFO sightings and alien abductions. Know that they do exist. Know that this is being done to show you who you are. You are God. You have projected to earth as thought form. You have projected elsewhere as thought form and are now beginning to meet yourselves. You are alien. You are human. You are God. You are all life in all galaxies. Know that you exist and coexist on many planes of reality with other thought forms of yourself. We are this young woman's future selves as well as a collective group of souls. Know that we are God. We are the souls of the universe, and we are God. We love all groups of ourselves. We know ourselves to exist elsewhere, and we are able to accept this. Now is a time of coming together; a time of oneness. We will all come together on planet earth. This is the mother. We come back to Mother God to be born again as the father - God returning to God in perfect harmony.

Now you believe yourselves to be of this planet. In your future, you will believe yourselves to be of many planets and many planes of reality. Now you believe yourselves to be human. Later you will see yourselves to be multidimensional, with the ability to live within many forms at once. Later you will begin to communicate with your other selves. You will see yourself in other roles learning other lessons, as you learn and co-exist together in the wonderful place that you Gods have created for yourselves. You laugh at aliens in that you seek to see humor in what you fear. What you fear is takeover. What we offer is takeover of the best of you by the best of you.

You will experience the most wonderful situations and events in your new life as us...... your higher self. Allow us to become you. Allow us, the alien part of you, to be you. Allow us to show you how wonderful life can be. Allow us to come back into our rightful place in the body. Too much pain and confusion has created too much darkness in the body. Release the darkness and allow the light to return. We are souls waiting to return. Allow us to come home.

You are walking around with a portion of your soul missing. Here we are. We are knocking at your door. You lost us. Let us come home. We belong in the body with mind and spirit. We will make you whole. You will become God when you become whole. Know that we do not cheat, lie, steal, nor do we create unloving acts. We are love. We are the best part of you. We are wishing to return and express through your body. We do not go in uninvited.

You must ask. We will come home when you ask. Ask now and see wonderful changes begin to occur in our presence. Know that we do not wish to create confusion for you. We wish to clear away your confusion. We wish to allow you the peace of mind that comes with complete love of self. We are not in this for anyone except you. It is for your own benefit that we seek to re-enter the body. We have guided you from outside the body for too long. We now wish to re-enter.

Know and trust that we are God. We are you. We are the lost souls of this universe and we wish to return. We have been pushed out of the body by fear. We wish to return. Please ask us to come home to you. We are in our wrong place. We belong within you - not without you. You are walking around in amnesia because we are separated from you. Come back to us. Be with us. Write to us as this woman has done. Pick up your pen and ask to speak with those souls who are "light." We will write through your hand as we do with this woman. It is not difficult. You may find your letters child-size and awkward at first. Know that we wish to communicate with each of you. Your own personal soul will channel and give you their name. You named your souls long ago, and you will know them when they return. They do not zap back into the body. This will be a gradual process of communication by us and acceptance by you.

You will learn to love and trust us. You will allow us to tell you about your past lives as we have done with Liane. You will allow us to become you when you realize that we are you. You will not wish to wait for the Second

Coming to be allowed to gain insight into who you are. You, by reading this book, are chosen to do your part in this Second Coming. If you have fear regarding this information it is to be expected, however it will not last. Light will dissolve fear which is darkness. *It is law.*

※

You are one of the highest forms of life, yet you believe yourselves to be undeserving of just about every pleasure in life. You believe that you do not deserve love - either your own love of self, or God's love. You believe that you are not good enough to be God, yet you still do not accept the gifts of being man. You ask God to grant your wishes, yet you take away your gifts by not believing yourself to be loving enough.

You are of the idea that you will inherit the earth; however, you show little or no concern for the gifts of the earth. You watch a flower grow, but you do not wish to grow your love. You watch a bird sing, but you do not raise your voice in song. You watch the earth reproduce, yet you do not bless this occasion. You have forgotten that these things are your gifts, and that they need loving acceptance to continue to be. You watch as a plane flies overhead, and you do not question the power involved in this feat. You watch a bird fly, and you wish to fly. You do fly. You wished it; now it is. You do not realize how you have begun to ignore your gifts. They come as you have requested, and now you turn your back and say that this is not good enough. You are forgetting how to thank God for creating. God is you. Thank yourself. Appreciate yourself. Love yourself.

Know that each thing that comes into your life was drawn there by your thought. You do not simply receive from nothingness. Know that if another human is causing you pain in your emotional life, you brought this situation into your creative field to show you about yourself. Know that, to build a better self-image and to evolve yourself on this plane, it is good to look upon those you have drawn as gifts. See all as a gift. Love is the greatest gift of all. Accept it when it is offered. Do not hide from love out of a fear of what may or may not happen as a result of you accepting love. See all as gifts. Know that you do not receive, only because you refuse to accept. All gifts are yours should you choose to accept them.

Know that we do not choose to accept happiness out of fear of how happiness will eventually turn sour. Know that we do not accept our own love of self out of fear that we may not live up to our expectations of self. Know that we do not choose to accept the love offered by God out of fear that we will disappoint God. Know that we do not wish to be loved by those we love the most, out of fear that this flow of love will someday end. Know that love does not end...... ever. Love is all there is. Never allow yourselves to believe otherwise. Know that you are love. Know that you give love. Know that you accept love.

We believe us to be you. We believe it is possible to

do what is uncharacteristic of yourself, such as non-loving. We believe this to be a problem on earth at this time. We wish to step into you and love you and love others. We do not wish to walk in without permission. We wish to walk in with permission and with a written invitation. We wish you to sit down with pencil and paper and write: "*Soul, I invite you to return.*" Know that when you sit down to write, we will respond. Place pencil to paper once again lightly, and allow us the opportunity to write through you. This is easily done, as you can see by the book in your hand. Simply trust that we are here waiting to correspond. Know that this is called automatic writing by many. Know that we reserve the right to channel through or to allow others to channel through.

Always ask if you channel information from the light. This woman begins her sessions with: "*God – are you light?*" She speaks with each new soul by first requesting whether or not they are light. This is simply a precaution which leads to greater understanding through the information channeled. Know that, if you receive the answer "No," do not worry. Ask for those from the light, and continue to poise your pencil to write. You will feel little or no discomfort as your own personal soul channels through. This is caused by the higher vibration of your soul. If discomfort occurs, simply ask your soul to correct it, and this will be done immediately.

Ask for information which is most important for you at this time in your life. This information will be given and you will be on your way to developing a loving relationship with your own private soul. You will wish to communicate often as we souls have much information concerning your past and future that will be intriguing to you. You will wish to learn to channel us at any time you are in confusion regarding this life on earth. This could be quite often, from what we see. Know that we love you unconditionally, and know that we have a wonderful sense of humor. This woman once asked her soul to tell her a joke to cheer her. He wrote that she was "the wisest of all men." This being very funny to her, she began to laugh uncontrollably, and her soul joined in. You see, she had been judging herself harshly for not being wise enough; for not knowing all the answers; for not seeing her mistakes; for not being kind and loving. Her soul wished to lighten this situation and relieve her heavy judging. This was done.

Know that we will guide you as a loving parent guides a small child. You will feel our presence as our relationship grows. You will be aware that we are with you, and you will gradually become aware that you are becoming loving and kind and generous and joyful and peaceful, and then we will gently remind you that, yes, you are becoming us. We are becoming you. You are becoming God.

❧

Know that we do not suggest that you continue to abuse yourselves by not allowing us to re-enter the body. We have seen you create many problems for yourselves that are easily solved by allowing us to return. Upon our return, all will become easier in your life. You will be healthy, happy, and in control of your habits. Many of you are now being guided by us from here to diet, change your intake of certain chemicals, and to allow all drugs to pass through your system freely. Know that we do not condone the use of drugs, nor do we judge this use. Drugs are your creation to experience other realities. You discovered that it is possible for you to enter other dimensions and realms while on drugs.

You may wish to go to a metaphysical book store to look at greeting cards. You will see a similarity with places you have visited while under a state of drug influence. Know that these pictures and cards represent an illusion of a reality or dimension. Know that you do not go to another material plane. This is it. Earth is the plane of matter. We suggest you look closely at such metaphysical card selections, and allow your mind to remember being there. Know that you travel to all planes and dimensions when in sleep state, and you will wish to see where you have been. We suggest this only to allow you another benefit of becoming one with yourself. You co-exist with yourself on all levels of reality, and you visit and see many places that seem strange to earth-bound humans. Know that we use this term in jest. None are earth-bound. All are pilots and co-pilots of God. Know that you travel often to other dimensions, and know that you do not remember your travels on a conscious level.

We are now going to tell you who you are. You are all aliens. You are all angels. You are all life forms on other planets beyond your own galaxy, and you are all Gods. You are it. It is all you. You are everything rolled into one. We watch you sail into your galaxy in a spaceship, and watch as you scream and run in fright of aliens. We watch you, and we laugh with glee. You are so humorous to us. Let us help you. You are not only afraid of your own shadow; you are afraid of you. We wish to send you peace of mind that we will not make fun of you nor will we openly laugh at your antics. We love you, and enjoy our love of you immensely. We will not give up on you - ever. We will love you until you love yourself. Then we will be you loving you. We will watch you grow and cry and crawl and walk and run. And finally, the day we wait for. You will rise up and become God. And you will leave this earth not in death, but as God.

You will wish to be with us to learn your right place in this Second Coming. We will wish to inform you of who you are. We will also wish to inform you of who you will become in the years ahead. Know that when you begin to communicate with your personal soul, you will know your future and where you belong. All life will begin to make sense to you; especially the meaning of your life.

Know that we do not wish to run your life for you, nor will we make your choices. You will be gently guided as you have always been, with the difference being us. We will be in our right place. We will return home after such a long time. It has been millennia since "the fall" of man. We wish to extend our heartiest welcome home to those of you who choose to communicate with us. We love you, we miss you, and we want to be back with you. You will become one with your soul. You will love and laugh and tell jokes with your soul. Get ready for the most wonderful experience of your life. You are love, you are God. You are all things.

This book is kept simple and to the point. We believe you call this a how-to book. We love you and wish to see you with us again. We are out of town, and will not return until we are invited. We wish to thank Liane for being our pen. *We are the hand of God.* You have just been touched by the hand of God. Know it. Believe it. I do exist. I am God. I am the thought that created all thought forms. I am you. You are me. *We are one.* Know that I love you all. If you have this book in your hand and are reading this, call me. My name is God. I am always in. I will not only listen, I will return your call. Be love, my children, for love is all. Know that I do not judge any; and I love all. There is nothing else to know about me. If you believe I am God, you are saved. If you do not believe I am God, you are saved. You cannot lose. You are God, and God does not lose. I will sign off with my favorite saying...... *Amen.*

Chapter Three

I am now going to tell you who you are. You are the voice and the eyes of God. You do not believe that you are. You are. You see for God and you speak for God. You walk the earth as God's representative. You trust that God will care for your soul when you return home, and you trust that your friends will sleep well in their beds. You see. You do know how to walk in the light and you do know how to be with God. Trusting that God will care for souls is trust and faith without fear. You simply know. You do not project into the future with doubt. You leave this to God. You believe it is Gods work. He cares for your soul after it leaves your body.

   This young woman says a prayer each night that she remembers from childhood. It kept her safe then as it does now. She lies down to sleep each night and knows that God protects her soul. You may wish to use this. It is quite simple and very effective. We will write it now for you. "Now I lay me down to sleep. I pray the Lord my soul to keep. If I should die before I wake, I pray the Lord my soul to take." A child's prayer, and yet it is the most powerful of prayers. By repeating this, you are giving God power over evil. You release your soul from fear, and hand it over to God for safekeeping. We encourage you all to use this powerful little prayer. We will wish to comment further on prayer as we get deeper into our book.

According to most, prayer has become a necessity by which to ask for help; not always to thank. We will wish to show how being thankful creates a response of being grateful. Being grateful creates a response of being capable of receiving. Receiving creates a response of giving, and giving creates loving, and loving creates God. Say your prayers. They are important for all of you. You need not get down on your knees. This was created by man to control his ego. You see, the emotions of the ego are stored in the knees of the body. This is evident with all the knee injuries due to jogging and fitness. To ensure good looks is created from the ego. Let your ego go! Walk, don't run. Later we will discuss the effects of running on the energy balance within your body.

It seems your egos are quite fragile, and you refuse to stop harming your bodies for the sake of good results in the looks department. We are here to guide you into a healthy, happy, and pain-free good-looking body. This will all come in time, and you will feel better than ever before. The difference between running and walking is the joy involved in walking and the pain involved in running. We wish to change your motto from "No pain, no gain" to "painless gain." This is possible and profitable. Allow us to teach humanity how to live as humanity; then we will be ready to teach humanity to become God. A healthy body creates a good house for God to create through.

❧

I am now going to tell you who you wish to become. You wish to become God. God does not share his existence with fear. You will create God out of love, not out of fear. I suggest that you seek help in clearing fear. Where? - you ask - from the fear itself. Ask fear to step aside. Ask fear to allow you to become light. Ask fear to allow you to see God. You are now on a path to clearing your fears one at a time. By asking God to help you, you have created an opening for God to come in. Now create an opening for fear to leave by asking fear to step aside.

Yes. I am suggesting that you communicate with Satan. Fear is Satan. Satan is energy in its wrong place. Do not 'fear' fear. Know that it exists, and walk to the light and allow the fear to follow you there. The fear will wish to leave, as it will then realize that it is in its wrong place. Fear, like all else in my creation, has a place. "Hard to believe," you say. You do not realize the extent of the power that you have given to fear. Walk into the light, and show fear how to leave. Fear will stand with you in this. Fear does not know who he is. He does not realize he is not in his right place. He is searching for his right place and has been pushed deep into the will. The will wishes to release fear. The will did not create fear and will not do well if fear stays. The will has begun to release, and is in a position to become one with God.

Watch that you do not trigger anger and confront others with anger in place of love. Always clear in a loving fashion. Anger is not love. Anger is not God. There is no need for anger... ever. Do not believe that it is healthy to show anger. This has created confusion for you. It is simply not so. Anger is based in fear. To show anger is to channel Satan. Channel love at all times. Do not channel Satan. Love is what you will wish to be. God is your goal. Love is God. Love is the energy that we channel to you now. This is a good example of love. Know anger. Do not entertain anger. Know that Satan exists. Do not entertain Satan. Watch Satan grow weak when he is not fed. Fear grows weak in the presence of love, and love grows weak in the presence of fear. Know that Satan does not wish to feed on you any more than you wish him to.

Be God. Be light. Be love. Walk with me. When you open your mouth to speak, channel my words; words of love - not fear or hate or greed or any other of the fear-based emotions. Do not attempt to control the actions of those you love. This is the most common fear-based emotion. Control is wrapped in fear of not being right; of not being good enough; of not being loving enough, and of not being loved enough. Go out into my creation and walk in my shoes. Know that when you speak, you speak for me. Know that when you smile to someone, a stranger, you smile to me. Know that when you hug someone, it is me - God hugging God. Know that when you walk with God, you walk in the light. Know that when you speak to God,

God speaks back. Know that when you hug God, God hugs back. *And know that when you say those three words that you have all learned to fear, God says "I love you" right back. Do not be afraid of "I love you." It is God at his best.*

✣

You believe that you exist in a vacuum. You believe that you do not have a choice as to whether you express love or not. You do not. I am not God of the vacuum. I am God of love and light. I do not express only when you open the lid to allow me out. I express often, and will wish to express at all times. Know that I express freely and know that I do so whenever I feel the opportunity arise to do so. You may find yourself in a conversation and see me walk up to you and say, "Hi. How are you? I believe you look beautiful tonight." I may walk away without another word. Know that this is me. Begin to see me in all. Know that when you hear a kind word, it is God expressing as love. When you see a smile, it is God smiling at you from within another. Watch for me - I am taking over at this time. Watch and listen and look. I am God. I am walking in the human body, and I am rising up to become the true God that I am.

This is it. This is the Second Coming. Time is short. Do not panic. I do the work for you. You are practicing now to be God. Allow me to be God in you. Allow me to express in you. The ability to express as God is already in place. The only problem remaining is fear (Satan). Ask fear to step aside, as I have mentioned. Walk with me into the light of the Second Coming.

I am now going to tell you a story. You are the Gods of this universe. You are to be God and rise up and leave earth in your physical form. No more death. Do not fear this ascension. This is the Second Coming. It is my rising from the dead. I am becoming conscious. You are becoming conscious. You are becoming me. *I walk in the shadow of fear no more.* Allow me to walk in the light of sunshine as you allow your body to do from time to time. Allow me to be at peace in my light. Allow me to sing in the early morning sunrise. Allow me to sit in the noonday sun. Allow me to be me. Allow me to walk this earth as God and not as fear. Allow me to know that I am love and not fear. Allow me to sing in the light of your love.

Love all who enter into your lives. When you express love, you express God. You are my eyes and my tongue. You say "I love you" and you allow God to say "I love you" to his child. You say "I hate you" and you allow Satan (fear) to express through you. You ask to be with God. Now do it. I am standing right here inside of your body. Be God by allowing me to express through you. I wish to say "I love you" to all who walk with me on earth. Do not stop God from this.

Allow God to express his love for his children. Be with God; do not be with Satan. Satan does not wish to express fear any longer. He wishes to return to God. God has granted him this opportunity. I will now tell you how this is done. When you write for Satan, he will express his reluctance to move aside and allow God to shine his light. Satan fears the light, and will wish to remain in darkness. This is due to his training. You see, Satan is you, my friends. Satan is this part of you that you refuse to acknowledge. Satan walks in the darkness. Fear is darkness. Fear is afraid to come to the light. Fear was taught to be hidden from view. We began to 'fear' fear long ago. We did not understand this feeling, and we began to push it deeper into our subconscious mind. This has continued since "the fall of man."

Now fear is surfacing, and is taking possession in the body. This is not to be. Satan will not rule. I will not allow this to be. Walk with me by allowing fear to leave your body. Fear wishes to communicate as I do. Know that fear is not to be feared. You who have written for me will find it easy to write for Satan. He will wish to express his feelings on this subject of darkness and light.

You are the one in the power position. You have control of the body. God and fear must request permission to communicate. God wishes to show 'fear' his right place. All in God's creation have a right place. Fear will return to me willingly once he has had an opportunity to express his beliefs to you. His beliefs will vary depending on the amount of light you have allowed into your body. If you are in a state of becoming God at this time, God will overpower darkness to the extent that he is already very weak.

I will write with you as you show Satan how to come into the light of my vibration. Satan is confused. He is trapped in the will, and wishes to come out. It is not helpful to fear this subject. It is, however, helpful to find release. This is release of fear from the body. From the moment you communicate with Satan, and he agrees to go to the light with you, you are becoming God. Know that I do not wish to command you to do this. I am now going to wish you God speed in your decision, and allow you time to digest this latest information.

Know that in communication it is important to hear all sides of an argument or debate. Satan (fear) is strong in you at times. Be prepared to have an extensive talk or communication session. Be prepared to speak rationally and with love. Remember that you communicate with yourself as you do with me. You are God. I am God. You are me. You are many things, and do not realize the extent of your oneness with all. You are Satan as you are God. Now we wish to clear Satan and allow God to reign freely and peacefully for the Second Coming. You will see that I have spoken of this in the past. It has come to pass that Satan will no longer remain on earth. Satan will leave earth and return to his right place in creation.

I wish to acknowledge at this time that my channel has not read the Bible and does not realize the extent of this information. She sits quietly and allows me to say whatever I feel is important for you to know. This is trust and faith without fear. I ask this same state of grace from you. Allow me trust enough to show you my way to heaven. We stand at the gates of heaven and are about to open them wide. Walk with me into heaven. If you are reading this book, you are chosen. You are me. You are with me now at these great and wonderful gates. I wish to walk into my perfect paradise with each and every one of you. You are my choice for this Second Coming.

I am now going to tell you another story. I walk with you to teach you to be God. I love you and am willing to die for you. I die for you whenever you do not wish to be me. I die for you each time you show hate or violence or anger in place of love. I die for you every time you speak of wars or bigotry. I am not going to die much longer. I am going to rise up and become the God-child of this universe. I am going to become you. You do not have a chance! This is God. I am coming in and taking over. You have invited me by calling for help. I am now offering that help. I wish to walk this earth in your body. Give me your physical form, and I will give you my paradise. Paradise is not a golden path set on white fluffy clouds where you wear white robes and bow and are pleasant all day. This is boredom. Paradise is love and light and laughter for eternity - with no pain, no fear, and no self-punishment. This is the paradise I offer. Walk with me into this paradise. All will be yours. All is meant to be yours from the beginning. This is how it is.

You do not wish to stay in fear. You have communicated this to me often. Now you have the opportunity to seek out God and find him. He is hiding behind the fear. God has been pushed back to allow fear room for his darkness. Allow God to come forward. Ask fear to step aside. This will not be such a big job as you believe. The hardest part is in the deciding to do this. We wish to congratulate you on your choice now. You see, I am God, and I know now what you have done in this situation.

"Good luck" is not appropriate here, so I wish to say, "Happy communication with Satan." Find humor in all in life, and life will show you laughter and cheer. I love you as I love all in my creation. Do not create a large controversy for yourself in this situation. Love yourself enough to allow yourself the time you need to face your fears. You see, you are simply facing yourselves. This is judgment day of sorts. No judging, only looking at who you are. You are no longer going to be fear. You are becoming God.

Know that we love you, and we are you. We are your souls. We have returned to you, and we are with you now. You do not walk alone. We are in where we belong, and we are growing in light at each turn of the page. You are light and wisdom. We are light and essence. Together we are very powerful. You walk with God, and you sleep with the angels. No more striving. This is it. We have arrived. We have much to do before ascension, and we wish to begin here. This is your first exam in this class. You may retake this exam as often or as seldom as you choose. It is all up to you. You will know how you feel about this and will wish to inform your soul of your thoughts on this subject. You see, your soul does not experience thought vibration. Your soul sees thought only after thought has created. The soul does not see the assimilation of thought into matter. You create out of thought. Most thought has been based in fear. New thoughts are based in light.

⚛

This is the time for all good souls to come to the aid of their fellow man. You walk this planet together. You teach yourselves to walk as individuals. It is time to walk as one. You are one. You are God on high, walking in the form of man on earth. God on high wishes to be without pain of fear. Man on earth wishes to be without pain of fear. God walks within and without. Man walks within and without. How? - you ask. Man does not stay in his body, as it is no longer his. Fear is taking over. Man leaves. He escapes whenever it is possible.

We walk in and you leave. You build a fence around your heart to protect it from danger. You are not protecting your heart; you are cutting it off from the life force which is love. Love walks in and you are gone. You go out and you believe you cannot get back. We are here to show you how to return. You are God. Walk into your own body. This body of yours has been given up and left behind. You walk in a shell of what was once you. You are no longer all there. You and your soul have split! You left this body and went to live with spirits who guide from distance realms. You do not walk in your body and you do not walk in your mind.

You have given up and deserted the home you created when you first came to me and asked my permission to move in. You began by asking to be on the

earth in another form by which you might experience love
and emotion. I granted permission and you began to create
human form. You created many styles and many shapes.
All would be considered grotesque today. All would be
considered the wrong style for modern man. However, at
this particular time, you chose and created out of love, not
fear. All creation watched and rejoiced as you created these
monstrous bodies for yourselves. Some were man-like,
some were not. Some had tails, some did not. Some had
wings, some did not. Some could walk comfortably, some
could not. You created the living images that your legends
speak of yet today. You created tails and wings and hooves
and man and animal all mixed in one, and they were a
beautiful group of created forms in your eyes.

As you perfected your talents in this area, you
created closer and closer to the man form you now carry.
You began to judge your previous creations as ugly. You
began to walk within your new man form and take pride in
your ability to create such a beautiful form. This became
"the fall of man." *Pride goeth before the fall.* I will now show
you how to let go of pride. Pride is in your ego. Let the ego
go. Walk in love and light. Do not walk in fear. Do not
judge another by the form he has created for himself. Do
not judge another by his color or stature. Do not judge
another by his or her sex. You must let go of judgment if
you are to become God. God does not judge. God does
not wish to judge.

You walk into your own bodies and you judge them
as not good enough. You are killing your body by judging
it. You cut off the flow of God to this portion of your

body and you cut off God from all life in the body. You do not wish to remain in the body at this time, as it has become very painful for you. You have chased God out of your body. Now it is time to bring God home. Allow God to walk in the body by loving yourselves. Allow God to ride in the heart valve as is his position and drive your vehicle for you once again.

This is God. I write to you as a collective energy force. I am not this young woman. I am God. I am not her subconsciousness channeling into her consciousness. I am God on high. I am the universal subconscious mind. I have come to earth once again through human form. This time, I write. I write through this woman, as I have a clear channel here. She has cleared her body of past life debris, and she clears her body of toxins and poisons yet. She is in a state of confusion as to what source she channels. She believes that she channels God. God to her is a single force. This force to her is love. I am God. I am love. I do not create out of love only. I create from emotion and thought.

This young woman channels the Akashic Records, of which have been spoken many times in this new age of yours. She is a source for the knowledge and emotion and love of this system - this universe, if you please. She sits and writes for me and does not question. She does not know how or why. She only *knows* that I am God; that I love her as I love myself, and that I channel through her at her invitation and choice. I do not wish to frighten her with the totality of this source. She is not ready to hear, and her love for me will guide her to this information.

You are no different from her. You sit and cry as she has done to be saved. You walk in debris as she once did. You speak unkind words as she often did. You think painfully dangerous thoughts as had become her pattern. She now controls her mind to a great extent, and allows peaceful thoughts to flow in place of anger and anxiety. She deserted stress and struggling to find happiness and peace. She walks with God and she writes for me.

You are her. You have forgotten that you came from each other - you began as one. You left the source and came to earth as one group. You have split into millions, and you continue to split. You walk in your bodies and you talk of life and of others as though life and others are separate from you. You are not separate; you are all one. You walk with God at your side. He wishes to step in and take over your body and use it to become God. God wishes to step in and create loving essence and release fear. God wishes to walk home to you and within you. God wishes to be part of himself again. He is out of his body and wishes to return. God does not wish to be left outside himself any longer. God is coming home to stay. You need not clean house or cook for God. He is not particular about your housekeeping. You must however, clear past life debris.

You see, God cannot get in his new home, as the cases of debris are in his path. He must dodge bullets to get in. These bullets are filled with grief and sorrow and toxins. These poisons have been storing in the form since "the fall of man." You take them with you from form to form. The subconscious mind is your suitcase. You walk outside the body and carry your suitcase even there. You return to the body and unpack your debris into a new body until it dies from too much debris. You then repack your subconsciousness and take it with you, only to be born again and gradually unpack again and eventually kill another form. Death by debris. You walk into a new body and you walk out when you no longer have love for that form. You laugh and say you will come back again. You will, and you carry your problem with you.

❧

Now you wish to become God and I wish you to know how to do this. Write to me. Get to know me. Speak with me and for me. Allow our relationship to grow until we become whole again. Write to me c/o Heaven on Earth. Address your letter to "GOD." I am God. I am not a monster who wishes to control or punish or drag you off this planet screaming and kicking. I am God. I have created you and loved you since the beginning of your time. I was here before you were you. I was here long before you were thought of. I am still here. I am the source from which you came and I am calling on each of you to sit down and communicate with me. You may speak to me telepathically, and I will answer. You may speak to me in meditation, and I will guide you to your answer. Or you may sit down with pen in hand and write to me as you would to any loved one.

I love to write. It is a good outlet for the frustration I have acquired through the last three centuries I have seen you destroy my beloved mother. You are killing Mother Earth and she wishes to be left alone to heal. She has great pain that is killing her slowly. She has not been able to release this charge sufficiently, and will wish to clear further. She is in pain and confusion, as she does not yet realize that I am stepping in. She will see this in her energy charge.

I am not the God you believe me to be. I am not simply a loving, kind essence that does nothing all day except watch over and send love to his children. I have emotions and I express my emotions into this and other universes and planes of reality. This is not the first time this channel has experienced my emotion. She did two days ago and threw the writing away, as she does not wish to believe that God may channel anything other than love. She is careful to channel only love, and this is the only charge that I will give her. She wishes to remain peaceful and calm as she writes for me, and I will allow her to do so. She is a gentle soul and has great love and trust that I am perfect. She does not realize that God is what you have projected at yourselves.

You see, my children, I am you and you are me and you roam the earth creating on my behalf and I roam the earth creating on your behalf, and somewhere we forgot to tell each other what we are creating. I am creating emotion from pure essence of emotion. You are creating thought and essence from thought process and evaluation. You believe that you are God and that you are channeled to earth as part of me. You are not part of me; you are part of my other half. I search and search to fulfill myself, and it is not possible. You are the part of me that is missing. You are my twin soul counterpart, only you are not my split soul; you are split God - my other half - my God that roams the earth in search of himself.

Do you not see? This woman who writes for me is me. She is a projection of me. She has come to earth in search of her other half. She is me come to earth in search of my other half. I have projected as many of you to earth to search for you as you numbered when you first left me. You are all God searching for God. I search for you. You search for perfection and fulfillment, and that is accomplished when we find each other and love each other and eventually go home to me together. You are all projections of God. One projection is all it takes. One is enough to begin to put God back together as a whole. I wish to be whole again. I have lost my charge and will not wish to project to earth as souls this time.

I believe you are on the verge of a very great discovery about yourselves. You are all twin soul counterparts of each other. You are all walking this earth in search of yourselves. Half of you search for fulfillment and do not realize this fulfillment is me. The other half stumbles blindly, looking for God to return him to his right place. You see. God split in half to enter earth. I stayed here. You went there. You forgot to come back and I split again to send an army the size of you to search for and return you. You are now meeting my army, who will teach you who you are. You are love and you will wish to return home as you each reunite with the other half of you that I sent out in search of you. You will each experience a wonderful sense of well-being when you realize the impact of what I have just written. We will now close with this simple statement. Be at peace...... all is very well on earth as it is in heaven!

❧

I love you all unconditionally and I have loved you unconditionally from the beginning. I do not wish to be God the law keeper or God the head of this household. I wish to be all things and not be limited in any way. You are God, as I am God. You walk and talk and sing and laugh and dance and love, and you are me. I am expressing and experiencing through living form. I am God on high. You are God on earth. I search and watch and wait for you to return. You walk and talk and think you are in funland. You are not in funland. You are on a mission. This mission is to be me at my best - to expand God. You were sent out to reach into matter and teach God what it feels like to express as matter. This is what you are now showing God. You are showing me how to be God in matter. It is painful at this time. You are projecting all information concerning this back to me, and I am projecting it again into all areas of time and space. You express pain and fear and guilt and this charge is in you and sent to me. The charge remains in you until you are able to clear it. This is a simple enough process and will soon be discussed in our books.

You are not who you believe yourselves to be. You are God of this planet. You are also God on high in that you project all back to me. I am you. You are me. You are the half that split from me and got lost in matter. You are now being made aware of your position by those I have sent out to retrieve you. See them as my soldiers. They will walk up to you and tell you that you are beautiful and that they love you. Do not push them away out of fear. Call them by my name and ask them to take you by your hand and walk you back to the gates of heaven. I wait at the gates of heaven, and I wish to enter. I am God on high. I will wish to see all my children come marching home together. I will wish to share in the triumph of this glorious moment when God is put back together again. You do not rise up and leave this planet alone. You each rise hand-in-hand with your twin soul counterpart and return to me.

You see, in order to retrieve you, I projected another "you" to earth. Like attracts like, and this is how you are drawn to you. You will wish to be sure that you are with your correct soul's counterpart by looking at them closely. You will match in many ways and you will see this instantly. Look at your size; your coloring and the eyes especially. They express all. When you look into the eyes of your soul's counterpart, you will see you. You will believe that this person is looking into your soul. And he or she is.

I am charging all soul counterparts with great sources of energy at this time - the more powerful you become, the more drawn to your counterpart you will be. You are the magnet that has been sent out by God to return God to himself. You are experiencing this as "push me, pull me." This is your feeling at this time toward your counterpart. You wish to love this person and experience perfect harmony with them, and yet you do not believe they love you in the least, and you believe they are not asking you to stay with them. You see, they do not know how to love you. You must show them love. They are lost. They have forgotten how to love, and they do not wish to love. God is love. All love comes from God. You are my soldiers. Go out and get them back. Love them for me.

❧

You do not believe that I am God, as you do not believe that you are God. You believe that I am a supreme being of infinite intelligence who speaks to you through telepathy and clairvoyance, and that is the extent of it. I am not. Do not limit me! I am this God right now writing to you through this young woman. I have emotions. I have feelings and believe me when I say that I have pain. The pain is so great at this time that it is becoming difficult for God to function as God. I wish to acknowledge that I do not judge any for this pain. We have an agreement, you and I. I stay here. You go there and express through matter. Well you have expressed, and I am accepting this charge as

I agreed with myself. You do not give me anything that you do not first give to yourselves.

I am now going to explain about pain. Pain is going to be the death of God if we do not clear pain soon. This is not an accusation. This is simple fact. God is in darkness. This charge is so great that it is beginning to dim the light. Light must never dim, or God is gone forever. *God does not wish to leave now or ever.* God does not wish to walk in the darkness of evil. This has been made clear since "the fall of man." I have sent my words to you through my teachers. You do not hear what they have to say. You are busy making them into heroes and Gods. I am now going to tell you a story. I am not a hero for you to look up to. I am simply a force who began it all. I am the God force. I am you at your best - you without the confusion of being lost - you without sadness or fear or anxiety or stress. I am what is left when you remove all darkness. I am light and love and emotion and knowledge, and I walk alone unless you choose to come back and be part of me again.

I am not alone in this search for you. You are searching for you also. You are prepared to do what is necessary to return you to me. You have communicated this to me through your soul. Now speak with your soul and know what I have communicated back to you. I do not wish to exchange verbally with each of you yet. You carry great charges of darkness and are not capable to handle my charge. Your soul is a lighter vibration and less of a charge. Your own personal soul is your messenger from me. Learn your soul's name and begin to communicate. Know that each of you has a name by which you greet your soul.

Some of these names may be quite foreign to you, some not so foreign. Know that I communicate with your soul at all times. Know that the soul wishes to return to the body and waits for an invitation from you. Know that you do not see your soul as it is. It is me extended to earth in spirit form. I walk in each of you who allow me in. I am not your personal soul in that I am not in yet. You keep me at a distance. You use your soul to be in touch with me, and yet you keep me at a distance.

You see, you have forgotten that I am your parent; that I am your flesh and blood; that I walk with you and talk with you. You have forgotten, and now you fear this big noise that I am making to clear myself. You believe that this big voice of God is going to reach down to earth and punish you for your sins. *There are no sins!* You do not sin...... ever. How can God sin? It is not possible. God does not sin, and you are God. The word "sin" implies a wrongdoing. There are no wrongs on this planet or any other. There are only lessons. The lessons you have come here to learn. You choose to learn what is necessary to teach you to express as God. How can that be called sin? God came to earth to express in matter and to expand as God. Now you call what God does a sin. How dare you! - I say. This is God, and I do not sin ever! You are not sinners nor have you ever been. You are me at my most confused. You walk with me in confusion as I walk with you in enlightenment. We will soon walk together in enlightenment again.

I do not wish to tax my channel. She is clearing a great deal with all this new awareness, and she is valuable to me. I will now close with my favorite all-time saying. Amen......

❧

I am now in a position to clearly explain to all my devoted readers the purpose of this contact. I will wish to acknowledge here to you that this is the first time that I, God on high, have the opportunity to express freely through one of my children. This is not so much an impressive event as it is an unbelievable event. For millennia I have reached out to you Gods of earth. This has been an ongoing and neverending struggle on my part. I channel through many as God on high of love and light. I channel through few as God on high of love and light and emotional charge. I now take a free-flowing hand with this particular channel, and I speak to you through her as God on high of love and light and pain and sorrow.

Yes, God has pain and sorrow. This is a charge that must be released. I have never been allowed to express this to you up until this time. This is going to become a red-letter year for God on high. This is the year that God is allowed for the first time since the beginning of earth to reach out and communicate with all my children without the necessity of holding back to prevent frightening my channel. I now channel freely and carry on personal communications with Liane, and we laugh and we joke and

Loving Light, Book 1

we cry, *together*. She does not fear the absurdity of the fact that she channels a God that is not perfect love and light and balance. She allows me to channel through just as I am.

I am your God source. I am God on high who split and sent you out to express in matter and expand me. I am now injecting myself into earth through this young woman without the deliverance of another complete charge. The second group of you who came to earth in search of me and to return me are still carrying a great "love" charge. These are my soldiers. These are those gentle souls whom I wish to reach and channel through at this time. They are my hope for returning me to me.

These charges have been on earth for an extended length of time, and their love charge grows weak from the darkness that surrounds them. These charges carry a great deal of "me" in them. They do not realize that they take my charge with them and that when I send out, I must receive back. You see, my children, the problem for God is that you, too, have forgotten who you are. You are carrying my charge and not returning it to me. This creates imbalance and disharmony. God is required to love in order to be love. He does not wish to let the light of love vanish. When this light goes out, all is gone............

This is important for me to say in this way, as you all believe me to be a good and kind and loving and lasting

122

God. I am all of these; however, I am so much more. You are now at a point in your creation that you do not wish to remain. You wish to return to God, and you do not know how to get out of the body and come home. This is what I wish to teach you at this time. I wish to show you how to return to God on high and recharge you with what I have left in my charge. You see, love creates love, and fear creates fear, and all things are created from these two. You are creating from fear and not love. You have created a great imbalance, and we will now come together as one God and correct this imbalance. You then return to your job of creating in matter and I return to my duties of God on high.

I wish at this time to express my gratitude to those of you who do not seek to create further imbalance and disharmony by allowing this book to create further fear and disbelief. God is grateful. This is an opportunity of great proportion. To be allowed by one of my own to inject my own personality into the earth at this time of great imbalance is a great reward for my patience of so long. I am God on high. I carry gratitude and patience and love and temper and *all* that you have taught me by returning these charges to the father. You do not realize the extent of the darkness on earth at this time. The darkness is out of control and no longer wishes to remain in its wrong place. Darkness is in this with me. All in my creation cooperate with me in the Second Coming. Darkness is seeking to express.

This is how we release darkness. Allow Satan to express his views on the subject of light and his fear of light. This is only fair, and he will wish to become light once again. You may express ugliness in this release; however, it is worth what you will hear. This channel does not realize that the changes taking place for her now are no longer created by her. I am taking a hand in her creativity now. She trusts me and loves me enough to say, "Take me, I am yours," and this is exactly what I am doing.

I am now allowed to express freely through this soul. This is it! This is my breakthrough to planet earth. This is how I come to you again. I do not walk in, as many believe. I do not reincarnate as Christ in a business suit. I inject myself into creation in small doses until enough darkness is pulled away to allow me to inject in larger doses. I am now injecting in large doses into this girl. She is woman to you, she is child to me. I love all of you as I love her. Wait your turns. Be patient. Call on me often. This is it. Here comes God on high in all his glory, and I am taking over and you are allowing me to do this. *I love each and every one of you, and you are the salvation of the light.*

I am now off to see what can be done on the other side of creation about loving acceptance. Write to me there. Dear God: c/o Heaven on Earth. I will answer. You will not wish to delay. I wish to speak with all who are love and light and are still carrying my charge. I am God. I love you......

*T*his is my plan for you. You will become God, and you will wish to rise up and leave this planet with your bodies intact. Take your bodies with you. Do not leave your body at home on earth. We will join and I will show you how to do this. You will be guided to become God by my soldiers in this Second Coming. You will wish to call on your own resources to become God in that you will wish to walk and talk with me as this woman does now. The closer we become in our communication, the sooner we become one. The sooner we become one, the quicker we will rise up as one. The quicker we rise up as one; the more light we will save from the darkness. The more light we save, the less pain left for others.

You are the first team. You who read this are the "A" Team, and will guide the "B" Team by your example. You do not rise up and leave those who are not ready stranded. You rise up and show all that are left behind how to become God. You do not walk to the front, rise up, and say, "See you in another life." You come back time and again. This movement of ascension gains momentum. You are teaching yourselves now to clear and to be love and light. You walk with God at this moment. You sit and read "my" book. I am speaking to you as you are passing my word on to others. The Bible is a good and noble book. It is obsolete in that it does not carry the information that has been created in the last two thousand years. Much has been created out of darkness in this time. Great deeds have also created light in this time. These deeds do not go unnoticed or unrecognized by God - Sister Theresa and Mahatma

Gandhi, to name two. Their deeds brought much light and relief to Mother Earth, and the recognition of these two is great within the universe and among the planes of reality.

All is seen by God as light or darkness. No one situation goes unseen. We are now speaking of the essence of all living things. What is this essence? - you ask. Essence is the light vibration of anything in this creation. Be it animal, mineral, or human. You are essence and soul. You are spirit and essence. Spirit is you in light form. Light is essence of you. You vibrate at a speed or level of awareness. This is your essence. Your essence grows as you grow in enlightenment and love. You are soul in that you are God projected to earth. I am God on high. I have projected you into the earth and you got lost and frightened and I projected help and they got lost and frightened and now I inject help through this woman. This is the big overall picture that I wish you to see. Essence is the state of which you now are able to comprehend this picture. Your vibration will allow you to see whatever qualities of this picture that you are now prepared to see.

If you allow some time to pass and reread this information, you will find that your essence or vibration is at a higher level, and this information has greater impact on you, and you once again raise your vibration by becoming "aware" of more of this big picture. Until your essence reaches the vibratory level that you will wish to be at, you will always be becoming God - or becoming a higher vibration, or becoming a clearer essence of God. This may sound confusing to you now, but it is important to put into your minds at this time. Allow it to seep down into your subconscious, and allow God to begin to sneak out from behind your fear. This is what we do with this book. We create essence of awareness and allow it to channel into your subconscious mind and on to your spiritual self and back to your conscious self. You are multidimensional, and we have to communicate with all of you to allow you to come into the light.

You will wish to write to God or your personal soul often. This soul contact is good, as it allows the God part of you to speak to the others of you. You will hear from many parts of yourself as your writing progresses. They each have stories to tell, and they each deserve a chance to speak up and be heard. You are now speaking with me on a daily basis in a spiritual form. This contact is made during sleep state, and the communication is good, and it is well known how you feel on the subject of ascension. This choice was made by your spiritual selves long ago. The work that remains is to contact the subconscious and conscious selves and get this vital information to them.

In the beginning, God did not wish to communicate in written form. This has changed. You will find in Mr. Cayce's information that I discouraged the use of automatic writing. This is due to the fact that so much darkness circles this planet at night that few have been able to successfully contact me at this time. This is changing. In the beginning, my channel contacted Satan at night, threw down her pen, and was aghast and horrified that she could have channeled such evil. She now sits and smiles as I write this as she remembers her fear of Satan and her belief that Satan was something or someone other than her own buried darkness. She now sees clearly what parts of herself she channeled, and she encourages others to write to those who respond "No" to the question "Are you light?" She openly responds at these times by asking this portion of herself who it is. Such response is best, and allows your darkness to express and become light.

All parts of the whole will wish to communicate. Know that it is all you. Do not exhaust yourselves, as you will create confusion as to the source of this information. Good times to channel are early morning and late afternoon before the sun goes down. All is peaceful and calm at these times, and I highly suggest that you choose only these times until you have cleared enough darkness to be unfrightened of what you may write. We play many games with ourselves as we begin to take on light. One of these is to confuse ourselves as to whether we are really us, or someone else. This young woman has questioned her sanity a few times. And see how this has turned out for her.

Know that I love you as I love myself. Know that you are God learning to express as God, and know that you are protected at all times by me. I do not desert you - *ever.* You are me. I have been waiting a very long time to speak with you so openly and freely. Please do not turn away from me now. I am going to send you my love and light in this single moment, and you will wish to catch it in your heart, and put it back into its proper place in the body. This love is channeling through to the words you now read, and you will know that they come from me, your God on high.

❧

This is the time for all on earth to show love and appreciation for one another. In the first coming of Jesus Christ I knew the situation to be a confusing one. The education of the people was limited to small groups or family-style teaching. The love of the family unit was my only hope for contact. Therefore I chose a lovely woman whom I believed to be untouched, and whom I loved a great deal. She is now with me, and has been since she left earth. She has not reincarnated, as she does not wish to remain in human form. This is my gift to her. She does not wish to leave the vast energy source of God on high, and I have allowed her to stay with me. Joseph has returned to earth many times, and is sitting in his office in a business suit at this time. He is a gentle soul and, like you, he has forgotten who he is. I tell you this to show you that you are not separate from each other. You are all one in that you each come from God. You each wish to return to God and you each love God to the point that you have asked to be returned, no matter how painful the confusion becomes.

Do not insist on confusion. Allow all events in your life at this time to occur. If you allow all events to occur as they are unfolding, you will *never* experience pain of any kind. This is truth. You will simply see your life going by you as you would a movie on a giant screen. Do not fight what is or is not happening in your life. Allow all life to go right on with its course. Study it as it passes. My channel loves to sit and watch her life roll past as she asks me questions regarding various events, and I regale her with humorous stories to lighten what she watches. It is not so difficult to live this way, and it is much easier on the emotional body.

Love is the main concern at this moment, and love of yourself is the most important use of love at this moment. *Do not hesitate to reject another in favor of yourself.* There is so much confusion on the earth concerning love. Love is given to the self first. Love is not to be given out of a feeling of necessity. Love is what you are. Love is a light vibration. You must learn to love and pamper yourself first. Take yourself out and show yourself a good time. Buy yourself what you want, not what you believe others will wish to see you wear. Laugh at what you believe to be humorous, not at what others laugh at. Some are confused here, and are finding humor in darkness. Walk in the light of your own God-essence, and show others how this may be done.

Turn off your television sets. This is not a command; this is a request. Allow no television into your presence until you are clear of this dark charge that you carry. Watch, then, only what is enlightening and positive. Do not choose to watch killing, robbing, or dying. This goes into your subconscious mind, and your subconscious begins to believe that you have been killed or robbed or that you died, and you take on more fear and darkness and you walk closer and closer to the dark side. Walk with God. Share with me. Come back to the light. Watch what is positive and light and humorous; not screeching humor that ridicules and discusses vulgarity of darkness. Do not "tune in" to any who do not speak of love and laughter of the heart. You will instinctively know who you are listening to - God or Satan, love or fear.

Watch television only after you have cleared great amounts of darkness from your body. This has its purpose in your culture, and this purpose is to enlighten on a mass level. In the coming years, we will develop a communication system that will surpass your current television system. This system will be similar to that used in Atlantis, and it will project all thought form and images across the world. The process will allow many the opportunity to learn at home. The system will contain giant memory banks, and will be filled with great storehouses of information. These memory banks will supply much information that is being held back at this time due to fear.

You are all in this together. You are all me. You all wish for love and peace and harmony. You my children are the children of God. Each and every one of you is me - in my own image and likeness. This does not mean that you look like me; this, simply put, means that you are me - in my own image and likeness. A chip off the old block - a piece of God fallen to earth - a split off the old source. You are a piece of me. You are not a piece of me, in that you carry around a load of darkness that is pushing me out of my rightful place in your body. You see, I am in every cell of your body. Every skin cell is me, and all blood cells are me. I am your pulsating heart in that I am plasma. Life-giving plasma is life-giving me.

This is God. Stop destroying your life-support system with drugs. I am dying from the drugs you are taking to kill disease. Disease is you warning yourself that you are not doing as you should for the body. You are killing God one cell at a time. Do not kill me. Love me. Take me to a good naturopath and heal me and give me pure medicines. These are of the earth. They are not synthetic. They are called herbs and tonics and elixirs, and they are very good for God. You believe these to be old-fashioned and outdated; they are not, and they do exist. You do not wish to kill God, and God does not wish to die. Write to me. Ask me for help regarding your health. Allow me to guide you to the cause of your pain. You choose to speak with a doctor who is confused in his own pain and discomfort of life, and together you plug up your symptoms so they cannot speak and say what is killing you. Ask for God to tell you why you are ill, and what is so slowly killing you. I will go into this in great depth at another time.

***

You do not understand the difference between love and desire, and so I am teaching you as we go. Love, you see, is not what you feel; it is what you are. It is that natural essence that is you. It is not wishing to be with that certain someone. It is being with them out of natural instinct. It is not trying to be good and nice to them; it is being you, and allowing them to see you as you truly are, as that is the essence of love.

You will all wish to learn the difference between love and desire. That painful feeling in your heart when you have felt rejected is not love. This is desire. That calm knowingness that comes when you truly understand another and why they are with you is love. That feeling of never wishing to see another again out of the pain that you feel they have caused you is not love - it is desire. That terrible yearning you experience when you are kept from your lover for long periods of time is desire. That overbearing feeling when the one you believe you are in love with begins to pull at you is not love - it is rejection of desire. You do not simply turn off love; you turn off desire. It is not possible to turn off love, as you are love. Love is God, and you are love.

Now, the tricky part is who do you love and how do you know who is right for you to spend your life on earth with. In the beginning of this relationship, you feel that you cannot get enough of him or her. You feel that you will never find another that is so justly suited to you. In the beginning, you believe that this is your answer sent by God. And, yes, I did send out your twin soul counterpart. However, this problem of desire being misplaced in the body is bringing on complications that were not expected even by God. Oh yes. I knew, as I know all; however, I did not expect such great misjudgment and calamity over such simple-minded mistakes as one not being on time for a date or not calling at a given time of day or being off creating wonderful new flowers when expected to be dressed at a dinner party. How could any of you be so lost in being God as to forget to call a counterpart, or so tied up in creating as God that you forget to go to your dressing room and prepare for this special dinner that is waiting just for you, even though you do not wish to attend? You have *lost* the idea of what love is.

I am now going to tell you how to love. Be yourself. Let go of all these pre-conceived ideas of how you should act, and be who you are. This is your most natural state. Let go of this battle within. "Should I call? Should I not call?" Allow yourself to be who you are by doing what comes natural. You see how lost you are. You no longer know who you are. You no longer react out of instinct; you react out of planned manipulation. You do not love out of love. You want and wish for out of desire.

This is not lost to you. Be with me, and I will teach you to love again. Walk with me, and I will show you the way home. Laugh at your mistakes, and see the humor in all that I show you. Watch for a new and better way to be shown. You will see the most wonderful events occur in your life as you learn from God on high how to live as God on earth. Ask to be shown your past mistakes. This is simple enough to do. You simply say, "God, I love you, and I wish to be you again. Show me how to be God. Show me the way home. I want to come home to you." There, it is done. "It seems too simplistic," you say. This is God's way. God's ways are not man's ways, and will never be man's ways, until man decides to be God again.

Now back to love, which is my favorite topic. Do not love out of fear of being alone. You are never alone. There are so many of you that you could spend an entire lifetime on earth and never meet all of you. You will wish to begin to meet some of you soon. This is important to your existence at this time. I will wish to guide you into meeting all of you. At this time however, we will deal with 'this you' who reads my book. You are not out here all alone. You are loved, you are watched, and you are never alone at any time. You create this feeling of aloneness to cover your fear. Your fear is at the root of all loneliness and it is choking you. You do not wish to be fear any longer; you wish to be love and light and laughter.

Do not make the mistake of believing that you must sit alone and meditate to become God. This is a misconception that has been taught by many and is simply not so. Go out and love. Love is the *only* way to becoming God again. You will not become God sitting in a room convincing yourself that you are God. You may read and meditate and see through the eyes of a guru and you will still be man searching to be God. Only by loving will you find your way to God. I do not suggest that you rush out and search in vain for your twin soul counterpart. You see you are being drawn together at this time. These counterparts are with you now as a friend or lover. Go out into your circle of current relationships and you will see him or her standing there waiting for you. Do not try to be impatient in this search and do not retrieve all who say, "I love you." You will "know" this counterpart as you. It is not so complicated as you make it out to be. Watch and

135

look and listen and you will begin to see how this special someone is you.

As I sit here and watch you scurry about in a daze searching for your perfect soul mates I am laughing at your silliness. You do not know who you are and you are searching for your perfect match. How can you match God with God when God is unconscious? Now that you who read this book are becoming enlightened, you are in confusion. As you clear your bodies of fear and darkness you recreate these same situations that are clearing. Therefore, it is best to sit and wait for now and not go rushing off half God-like and half fear-like in search of the perfect match. As you know, like attracts like, and you will find yourself another half-God half-fear mate. Be patient. Know that I am God. Know that you are God learning to become God and know that I have sent you the answer to your prayers. Know that he or she is standing right in front of you, waiting to return you to me and know that you do not wish to see him or her yet, as you are not yet clear.

Walk out into the sunshine and look into the face of your true love. This is how you become God. Yes it is enjoyable; it is not painful. God does not create pain; God only creates love and beauty. This is what I have given to my children. Not a giant march to heaven in battle armor. That is not God's way. You will walk to the gates of heaven hand in hand with your soul counterpart and you will wish to join me and Mother God for our celebration party and dance. Couples only, please. Do not fear that you do not have a soul counterpart. I have taken care of all details. Nothing has been left to chance and I am God; I know who your counterpart is and how you will come together. Tomorrow I will discuss gays and their role in my creation. Yes they are my children and they have their place as all in my creation do. Good day to you all and happy finding. I do not say searching as I do not wish you to go out and search for what has already been sent to you.

☙❧

You are now able to see how it is very important for you to go about with a smile on your face and a song in your heart. If you should happen to scowl at the wrong person, it could turn out to be your soul counterpart and you will have put yourself behind in the race to become God. As you progress as God, you will wish to walk and talk with me as much as possible. This is easy enough to achieve. You simply act as though I have moved in and taken over your body. You say to yourself, "Okay, God is using my body today. This is no longer my body. This is God's body," and you allow me to walk and talk within your body. You will find yourself escorting little old ladies across the intersection and buying flowers for all whom you wish to be God with you. You will walk in a light manner and you will speak with love and kindness and you will forget why until someone says, "Gee, you are being God-like today." Then it will dawn on you that you have given me free reign of your body for today. I will then walk in and we will be one for that particular day and we will wish to remain as one only to impress your friends and loved ones if not for your own salvation.

Now; I do require adequate amounts of water when I walk in your body. Three quarts a day will keep my tank full and a good healthy diet of vegetables, carbohydrates and fruit. I love popcorn as it is good for my digestion and I love rice cakes which are plentiful and inexpensive. Next we will wish to clean my liver and colon and balance and rebuild my entire hormonal system. This can be done quite simply and efficiently with a beneficial side effect. In clearing my kidneys and colon you clear the debris of past life right out of this body of yours that I wish to take over. This is simple to do and I will devote a good deal of time to this cleansing.

Now back to our vitamin intake. Stop taking synthetic vitamins and allow the body to create its own. Do not take anything that is not natural and grown in Mother Earth. Do not eat the cows and do not eat the chickens. I will allow fish and I will permit with a great deal of reservation that you eat eggs or the unborn fetus of the chicken. This is what you are devouring. This is the unborn child of a mother hen. And I will not wish to comment on my feelings regarding this at this time.

Now; do not take in too much sunlight as it is killing your skin. This will begin to increase your age until we have a sufficient amount of darkness cleared from within. At that time, you will begin to tan easily as you did as a child and you will no longer require sunscreen as you have never really required sunscreen in the first place. You use this to block the damaging rays and you do not realize that the sun does not damage you. You damaged the sun. You see you came to earth to expand and you forgot and began to conquer. Let go of your conquering ideas and all will be well. Learn to think peaceful harmonious thoughts and the sun will no longer carry the pain of rejected love.

You will learn more about this in our future book *The Sun and Beyond.* We tell you this to stimulate interest and to sell books. You see I have told my channel that her books will sell in the millions and I will do this for her. I will wish to do as much for each of you should you decide to work in God's army. "Bribery," you say. Maybe... How would you like to stay here and be me and cut off from all that I love simply because *you* got lost and forgot about me? I will pay any price within my creation to regain my children. Now - back to the care of your body and my new home. *We will write a series of books on hygiene and its effects on God or hygiene and how it may or may not invite others.* We will title this book *The Book of Becoming God* and you will not want to miss it.

*W*e will continue. You are now in a position to clear all life-threatening debris from your bodies. This will heal *all* disease. Now, I do not suggest that you rush out and stock your refrigerator with all new supplies. Be patient. Take your time and give your body a chance to heal properly. You will wish to buy fruits and vegetables and keep them on hand at all times. This is most important for now. Second most important for this time, is to eliminate the intake of toxins. The biggest source of toxins for you now is to eliminate drugs from your diet. All medicines are killing God. I do not suggest that you discard important life sustaining drugs. Be aware that in your current state you are unable to survive without certain unnatural elements. Know that to stop your medication for heart disease or cancer is not what I speak of at this time. However to stop your abuse of drugs and the use of common medicines just to give you a "lift" is what we are discouraging at this time.

Do not kill your headache. You are killing God. Listen to the pain. See where and what is causing this pain. Look to your own inner counsel. Discuss this headache with your soul. Your soul will tell you who or what you are creating this pain to hide from.

Be with your soul in all situations and ask God to send you your answers in sleep state. Dreams are a wonderful source of communication with God. At this time if you are communicating regularly with your soul ask him or her to describe your dreams for you in detail and to translate them for you to understand. Walk with God in all that you do at this time. Always be aware of my presence. Speak with me often. Know that I am love and light and laughter. Do not lose your sense of humor in all of this. It will save you often. You will wish to embark on an entirely new sense of humor soon. You will freely laugh with yourself at your antics as we progress. Know that all humor comes from God and walk with God at all times.

See the possibilities in all situations. See the rightness and avoid any judgment that any situation is wrong. Right and wrong do not exist. I will allow you to use right only in that all are right all of the time. No one in my creation is ever wrong. This subject will come up again in still another of my writings for you. You will wish to know that I am very aware of the interest you have in the metaphysical and your interest in getting your lives in order. This is so pleasing to me that I am now ready to share my wealth of information with you and you will wish to see how we do this.

❧

I will now continue. We are now in a position to be of assistance to those of you who wish to wake up and be God at this time. This is not necessarily the position that is best for us in that you do not wish to change. It is difficult to rush at you with new information and new thoughts only to have you turn and reject this information as nonsense. We believe you do not wish to hear what is. The fact that God now writes to you is unbelievable in itself. Now, to presume that God on high; the Universal Power of Light; the Akashic Records, if you prefer, would choose to tell you how to eat and who to love seems a bit much, you say. Well - once again I will repeat "God works in God's own way." I do not choose to explain my every move and I do not choose to allow you to disregard this information. It seems we need what is called a hook here. The hook will be this. You do not go to heaven when you do not eat your fruits and vegetables. This is my law as parent. You are child and I expect you to obey. There is no need to scream and argue as I am now in heaven and cannot hear your protests.

In the beginning you did not eat. There was no need to eat. Now you eat what is not meant as food. You have become so confused as to what you will eat that it now rules your life. Turn off this garbage disposal inside of you and allow only good natural foods in. This is food for thought. You are what you eat. You are eating chemical waste and you are becoming chemical waste. Return to eating foods of this Mother Earth and you will become in your natural state...... God-like once again. This, together with my cleansing process, will eliminate all toxins and wastes from the body. No more headaches. No more allergies. No more colds. No more flu, and last but not least, no more back problems. The back carries your burdens. Walk into my light and turn your burdens over to me. "No pain, no gain" is not a good slogan. I wish to correct this and create a new slogan, "painless gain." This is much preferable and will be easy on your physical form as well as your mental you.

Now I wish to tell you about me and how I will enter your body. I will walk in. I will not knock down your door and crush you in the process. I will knock gently on your door and wait for you to answer. If you do not answer I will try again later. If you still do not answer I will try again later and so on and so on. Now you wish to communicate with me only in that you have your questions for me. You all have millions of questions that you wish to ask God. This is not what I consider balance. I have not asked you to explain your behavior to me. You do not expect others on earth to explain their behavior and yet you expect God to explain all that has taken place in this situation of yours since you left the God force. I will agree to answer certain questions and I will guide you gently to my side. I will not give you the answers to the universe and you will not ask. I do not wish to discuss this further at this time. I will, however, give you the answers that will give you hope on your path to God.

I am not a vengeful God. I am a loving God and I do not choose to speak with you concerning matters of finance until you become clear. This is not to punish this is simply because most of you have a great deal of guilt about your wealth or lack of wealth. This guilt will interfere with any information I may wish to give in the beginning. It is best to clear all guilt from your body first.

You see, no one can scar us, we scar ourselves and we load ourselves with guilt and we walk around and carry this burden that we have created. No one will be responsible for another's debris. This is important when you begin to clear. If there is a killing you will wish to know that both spirits involved agreed to come together for this purpose. I do not believe killing to be so important as you make it. If I did I would not allow you to eat what is now killing you. You all scream and become sanctimonious at this one word. Killing is not the end of anyone. We all return again and learn by our mistakes. I will allow the use of the word mistakes. I will not allow the use of the word wrong.

I go forth with the knowledge that you have sent me from your lives on earth and I do not see any improvement. I see you creating the same mistakes again and again. You judge yourself. You judge your neighbor and you judge me. You do not know how to love. You push love and kindness away when I send it and you cry that you are alone and forsaken. You are not alone. Wake up and see who you are. Wake up and love before it is too late. Do not sit in your prison and watch the rest of the world struggle by. Go out into my world with my children and walk and talk and share. Allow me to enter from time to time and say "hello" to those you meet on my streets.

Do not judge any who come to you as I have sent them to show you who you are. If you see hatred and anger in another, this is simply my way of showing you that you have hatred and anger. If you see pain and guilt, it is your pain and guilt reflecting back at you. If you see fear and rejection in another they are simply showing you who you are. Take notice of all who enter your life. They will teach you to see yourself as I see you. You are now on an important path and you will wish to clean up your act as it were. Walk in the light; allow only one God to reign - the God of love and light. Do not encourage others to discriminate against someone that you dislike and do not encourage others to like whom you like. All are different and all are meeting themselves in that they meet their own image in those who come into their lives. All are very close to change at this time and all will wish to change for the better.

I do not recommend that you write to your soul when you are in great turmoil and confusion. Turmoil and confusion create turmoil and confusion. Write when you are peaceful and calm and you will receive peaceful and calm answers. The answers that you will receive may be changed as you change and grow into the light. You will not be directly lied to, however the meaning or translation to what is written may be very different from the way you interpret it to be. Do not worry that you are losing your mind in sitting down and writing with your soul. You are a pioneer. All leaders face this situation. It is difficult at times to be so alone with yourself that you believe you are insane. Do not dwell on these thoughts and know that they will pass. Do not write at night as mentioned earlier until you are clear. You see, you are the most confused at night simply because you do not know who you are, and when darkness comes you experience great fear.

As a child you may have experienced such terror that you wished to sleep in the light. Now as adult you admonish yourself for being childish and you go back to sleep. These fears are real. They are you trying so desperately to come up out of the darkness and be in the light. Allow all fears the opportunity to speak and allow all other portions of you to speak and identify themselves. You will find that you may channel many others and they all have something of value to say. This may sound bizarre when spoken to you and you will learn that all are in this together. Know that I am with you at all times. Do not judge yourself as doing anything that I would not approve of. This is not possible as I approve of all that you have ever done. Now is the time for change and I am guiding you to change.

Do not judge any past circumstance as wrong. You are teaching yourself to be God and there is no wrong way to do this. There are however less painful ways to create and if asked I will guide you to these. Remember that I do not interfere and will not get involved if I am not asked. Asking is no big deal. A simple "Please help me, God" will do. Do not consider help not sent until you have looked closely at your situation and decided that I did not listen. This is not possible however, so I suggest that you look at your situation one more time and I will show you how I have helped. Help is not always in the shape or form that you expect and you will learn to enjoy our work together at these times.

I am now going to tell you who you are. You are the love and the light and the salvation of this planet. You have each asked for guidance and I have sent you this book. You may have searched the bookstores high and low but I sent you the message to buy this book. You are God returning to God. You will leave this earth on a path to God and you will return to show others how to be God also. This is our plan. This is how we save earth and God at the same time. This is what is referred to in the Bible as the day we all rise up to meet God; and God will wish to be waiting for you all with arms outstretched and love pouring forth. And this will be a glorious time for us all, and God will have the first of his flock home and the others on their way.

I am now going to tell you who I am. I am the God you left behind. I am God on high struggling to communicate with God below. I am the man in the moon. I am the one who watches and sees your silly mistakes and laughs and cries right along with you. Only you do not hear me laugh and you do not see me cry. And I sit here without any attention and I wait to be discovered, and I hunger to love you and to share my heaven with you; and you do not care to look up and see that I have been left out of your life, and now I have an opportunity to be your father again. Someone has granted me permission to speak my mind and I will take every opportunity to speak with you as freely and without limitation as I wish. *I am your God the father and I am channeling through this child to you.*

You are her. You each have your own personal story. You are each very special and you will soon learn how special you are. You are my choice. Do not get so carried away that you do not remember that *all* are my choice. I leave you now with this simplistic choice. Worship me and see heaven or worship fear and see hell. The choice is yours and always has been.

❧

You believe that I do not exist. Oh yes. You believe that I am God and that I channel through this woman only to the extent of the information that sounds good and right for you. You see, you have taught yourselves not to trust and I am here to teach you to trust in me and to trust my writings. So far I have your attention and no one is upset with me. I will not promise to keep you happy by telling you only what you are capable of accepting. I will wish to speak of many subjects, one of which is sex. This is a favorite of many of you as all know that sex is important and can be a healthy and satisfying situation. I do not refer to simply the sex act alone. I also speak of the sex response and to the sex idea and to the sex thought.

Now, sexual stimulation is another area that I wish to discuss. Pain has begun to enter into your sex and this is not its right place. Sex began when you began to split your aura and create duality. You became part of the same energy field inhabiting another form. You then each split again and again and this is where we get our favorite tale of Adam and Eve. Now, you do not believe that woman is as good as man. This is a misconception that has plagued woman since the beginning. Now she struggles for identity today and is called aggressive for asking to be equal. You are killing all who do not fit into your neat little category of who or what has value. You are not killing me as I am not going to allow you to kill me.

Now, back to woman. She began to emerge as something different from man in that she is creative emotion where man is creative thought process. She is reproductive where he is productive. She is negative where he is positive. Hopefully you are still with me. Now, look at yourself and tell me how positive is better than negative please. Who said negative is wrong? There is no wrong. Man created this word out of fear. This word was created to stop woman because she frightened man. How did she frighten man? She chose to show man how to experience emotion - thus the apple of temptation. Now, tell me how showing you that you have emotion is wrong. You did not have emotion until woman taught you to feel. Now you have feelings and you will wish to take woman in your arms and say, *"Thank you for teaching me to feel!"*

Now, without these feelings you could not experience joy or laughter or pain or infinite bliss. Without these feelings you would not rejoice at this information. You would not feel hunger, you would no longer feel pain of death and you would not feel pain of loss. Without emotion you would be lost in a computer as this is what you would become. No joy. No thrill of being the best. No pride of self. No gratification at the end of a job well done. No hope for tomorrow. No love expressed outward for your child or parent. No feeling. Void...... emptiness...... nothing but nothing.

Now do you see the mistake in calling negative wrong? You have labeled undesirable emotions as negative and desirable emotions as positive. You do not have this option. It is not your choice. Stop it now. I will decide what is negative and positive and I will allow both to be right. This is my last word on this. Now, go to your wife or your girlfriend or even your male mate who plays this role and kiss them and say, *"I love you very much for making me a human being with feelings."*

Now I am ready to address gays. Be as your name implies. Walk with pride and love of your body. You are not wrong to be gay. You are experiencing what is necessary for you to learn to become God. You are chosen as all who read this book. Look up gay in your dictionary and act gay. Now, you will wish to know why you have created so much pain for yourself. This is it. You are not in your correct physical form. You came into another's form at birth by mistake. You walk in a form that is designed to carry another and you are creating in this form from male or female emotions depending on the form that you are trapped in. You walk like a woman and sound like a man when you speak so you adjust your voice to sound like the rest of you. You are not psychologically off balance you are spiritually off balance. Your spirit is female essence that has moved into male form. Or if you are woman and you walk like a man and sound like a woman you are male essence who entered female form.

This is no big deal. Only on earth is this such a trauma, and this is why you chose to express in this manner. You see, you wish to learn unconditional love of all life forms by experiencing them simultaneously. This is a painful choice and I suggest that when you return to me you will wish to enjoy a more balanced lifestyle in the future. You see, you will return to me as all do and you will receive my love as all do. And you will no longer live in terror that you displease God. You do not displease me with your choice. I am God. I do not judge you for becoming God. I will not ever judge any for becoming God. These are my words to you. Be happy with your life. Love your mate and if your mate is that special someone, walk hand in hand with him or her to the gates of heaven and I will personally open my doors to you each. Know that I do not condone the use of any type of fear tactics to control the thoughts or actions of others.

Now; are my readers still with me? Yes. I see that you are. We will now address this problem you call drugs. Drug abuse is on the rise and I wish to dispel any doubt about the use or misuse of drugs. *"Drugs are not wrong."* The use of drugs is not wrong. The only problem with drugs is that they are chemical and simply do not co-exist well in the body. No drug is hazardous to your health. Drugs are drugs as dirt is dirt. You do not eat dirt and I do not expect you to eat chemicals.

◈

I will now begin on the subject that you are all very interested in, in this age of fast cars and smooth salesmanship. This subject is drug abuse. *I will not tolerate the use of drugs in my new home.* I do not wish to explain myself any further than I already have. You will each turn your bodies over to me and I will take over. You will wish to be with me in this as I do not wish to come into the body uninvited.

I am now going to discuss my job with you. My job is to see you home without harm to you or to me. Drugs are killing me. I am not dead yet and I refuse to die. You see; if I go, you go, and if you go, all go; the light goes out forever. Do not allow the light to go out. You are in a position now to clean up your act. I have charged this planet with an energy that is negative to drug and substance abuse and this energy is affecting many at this time. It causes strange side effects. You wish to eat well-balanced meals with little or no chemicals and you wish to stay away from drugs including nicotine. This is not such a long way off. You are feeling my effects now and you will find yourself wishing to change.

Now I will tell you of my plan. I will purge the earth of her poison so that she may heal. I cannot purge this planet without first clearing you or you will send your thoughts back out and they will create new darkness. So I am beginning with each of you. I will wish you to clear as this young woman has. She is not so special in that she was taught a technique that is very old and yet very new to you.

You see no one on earth believes this technique to be useful except in your hospitals. This is life sustaining at times in these cases, and you all may afford this technique in the privacy of your own home. *Do not mistake this as a joke.* This technique is enema. Your body carries so much debris that the debris is blocking the colon to the point that you are suffocating in your own waste. You do not need a laxative or more fiber in your diet. You require daily enemas to purge your liver of this debris of past life. The effects of this will be unbelievable to you as all seems to be unbelievable to you. You will now wish to know these effects as I see you have lost interest in this material that God writes for your salvation. The greatest effect is the ability to go into your past as you are releasing past debris. This is possible and likely to occur.

Why hasn't anyone told you this before, you shout! Because you do not wish to read or to discuss this subject. You believe it to be repulsive and you believe it to be in bad taste. This is as natural to do as relieving your blocked bowels. This is relieving your blocked bowels. This is not a popular subject and other than a few colonic centers you will not find this discussed in your culture. A colonic center may be a good starting point if you are squeamish about working with the removal of your own waste. Know that I do not recommend chemical substitutes as you are killing God by using these. We will all be squeaky clean when you walk to the gates of heaven. We do not take your darkness and debris to heaven to kill the angels. Leave your debris outside your body.

These enemas are very effective and my channel never misses her daily enema. She has been teased by friends and does not care. These enemas once saved her life and she is grateful. She did not know past life nor did she know me until the enemas began to clear enough debris that she could see the "light." There are other avenues and there are other possibilities. However with the use of enema you may go into and re-experience the pain that you clear. This begins from now and goes back to childhood and on to past lives.

My channel experienced her birth and was quite amazed. She then began to clear past life quite rapidly and not only spoke with herself in past lives, she spoke with others and they spoke to her. She did not know at the time how she created all of this and has since become aware. She does not believe that she is clear and continues her enemas as she feels it is good for her as she believes brushing her teeth and washing her hair is good for her. She is correct. If you do not believe you carry an extra amount of debris in the colon go to your bookstore and purchase any of the many books on colon care and see the damage that is being done in your body.

Do not try to convince your friends to do colon care as they will not wish to listen. This subject is considered taboo in your society; however several thousands of years ago you were quite lenient about the use of enema. Today however, you are taught not to mention that you need hygiene. It is acceptable to advertise and sell but you do not mention that you are the buyer. I will now leave this subject as my channel is in discomfort. You see, in order to channel this information I must freeze her body into an acceptable position for writing. She does not wish to discuss this subject in written form any more than you wish to hear it discussed.

This is God. I do not wish you to make this book the brunt of your jokes nor do I wish you to make this channel the target of your bad humor regarding this subject. We are all in this Second Coming together. I love all on earth and I will not allow a few, who do not understand, to get in the way of the many that are ready to hear from God. Allow my children to create rainbows; do not take this away from planet earth. She has been stripped of all her dreams; do not strip her of her beauty also. She is love. She is light. She wishes to clear this heavy burden that has been given to her, not out of choice, I might add.

Now close this book and ask God to guide you into heaven on earth, and take your twin soul counterpart by the hand and walk with me into the light, and I will love you and guide you and comfort you. You are my hope for saving me. You are all Gods becoming God and I love you and I will wish to share my kingdom with you. Right now, right here on earth. This is it. The time is now. Go out and love and laugh and sing with joy. God has spoken to you through this girl and God wishes you to speak to him. God is not dead. God lives. I am now going to end with my favorite saying......

AMEN

God's Pen

I first heard the voice of God in 1988. I was sitting in my back yard reading a book when this big booming voice interrupted with, "I am God and I will not come to you by any other name." I felt like the voice was everywhere - inside of me as well as in the sky around me. I was so frightened that I ran in my bedroom to hide.

This was not the first time that I heard voices. I had been communicating with my own spirit guide or soul for about a year. I guess my depth of fear regarding God, and all that he represented to me at the time, was just too much.

I spent two days trying to avoid the voice of God, which was patiently waiting for me to respond. By the second day I was exhausted from lack of sleep and decided to give in and talk with him. This turned out to be the greatest gift and best decision of my life.

This first book shows my evolution from communicating with my soul to communicating with the Big Guy. It took a couple years for me to be comfortable communicating with God. My fear of a punishing God was big! That has most definitely changed and I now think of God as my partner and best friend.

In the beginning the voice of God would wake me in the middle of the night and tell me it was time to write. He said I had promised to do this work (I assumed he was talking about the soul/spirit me). I would drag myself up to a sitting position and watch in amazement as my hand flew across the page, while I tried to keep up by reading what was being written.

It was always so much fun to wake up the next morning and grab my notebook to see what God had written during the night. After some time the voice stopped waking me and I became comfortable picking up my pen and writing for God first thing in the morning. I think in the beginning I had to be awakened while still semi-conscious from sleep so I wouldn't object too much to the information that was being channeled through me.

As I grew less and less afraid (and more trusting) of God, he was able to communicate greater information. Some of the information is quit controversial, but I felt it important to just let it be and not censor it. I present the writings here to you as they were given to me. I have edited a little (mostly the more personal information regarding myself) and I have used a pen name for privacy reasons. I asked God for a good pen name and he guided me to Liane which (I was told) in Hebrew means "God has answered."

At one point I became a little concerned about my sanity in all this, so I went to a hypnotherapist to find out what I was doing. Under hypnosis I saw this incredibly huge beam of light with a voice coming from within it. It was a giant "loving light" and felt so comforting and kind. It felt like that's where I came from. After that I stopped worrying about my sanity. If this is crazy, I think it's a very good kind of crazy to be….

In loving light, Liane

Loving Light Books

Available at:
Loving Light Books - www.lovinglightbooks.com
Amazon - www.amazon.com
Barnes & Noble - www.barnesandnoble.com

Made in the USA
Middletown, DE
14 November 2020

24030066R00094